T0327356

Measurement Madness

MEASUREMENT MADNESS

Recognizing and avoiding the pitfalls of performance measurement

Dina Gray
Pietro Micheli
Andrey Pavlov

WILEY

This edition first published 2015
© 2015 by Dina Gray, Pietro Micheli and Andrey Pavlov

Registered office
John Wiley & Sons Ltd, The Atrium, Southern Gate, Chichester, West Sussex, PO19 8SQ, United Kingdom

For details of our global editorial offices, for customer services and for information about how to apply for
permission to reuse the copyright material in this book please see our website at www.wiley.com.

Wiley publishes in a variety of print and electronic formats and by print-on-demand. Some material included
with standard print versions of this book may not be included in e-books or in print-on-demand. If this book
refers to media such as a CD or DVD that is not included in the version you purchased, you may download this
material at http://booksupport.wiley.com. For more information about Wiley products, visit www.wiley.com.

Designations used by companies to distinguish their products are often claimed as trademarks. All brand names
and product names used in this book are trade names, service marks, trademarks or registered trademarks of
their respective owners. The publisher is not associated with any product or vendor mentioned in this book.

Limit of Liability/Disclaimer of Warranty: While the publisher and author have used their best efforts in
preparing this book, they make no representations or warranties with respect to the accuracy or completeness
of the contents of this book and specifically disclaim any implied warranties of merchantability or fitness for
a particular purpose. It is sold on the understanding that the publisher is not engaged in rendering professional
services and neither the publisher nor the author shall be liable for damages arising herefrom. If professional
advice or other expert assistance is required, the services of a competent professional should be sought.

Library of Congress Cataloging-in-Publication Data
Measurement madness : recognizing and avoiding the pitfalls of performance measurement / Dina Gray, Pietro
Micheli, Andrey Pavlov
   pages cm
  Includes bibliographical references and index.
   ISBN 978-1-119-97070-5 (hardback) — ISBN 978-1-118-46451-9 (ebk) —
   ISBN 978-1-119-96051-5 (ebk) 1. Performance—Management. 2. Performance—Measurement. I. Gray,
Dina. II. Micheli, Pietro. III. Pavlov, Andrey.
   HF5549.5.P35M427 2014
   658.4'013—dc23   2014020919

A catalogue record for this book is available from the British Library.

ISBN 978–1–119–97070–5 (hardback) ISBN 978–1–118–46451–9 (ebk)
ISBN 978–1–119–96051–5 (ebk)

Cover design: Wiley

Set in 11/13pt Times by Laserwords Private Ltd, Chennai, India

Contents

From the Authors

Over the past 20 years, the world has witnessed a booming interest in performance measurement across all walks of life. Today, the vast majority of organizations employ at least some aspects of a performance measurement system, be it the use of key performance indicators to track progress, the setting of targets to motivate and direct attention, or the use of measurable objectives for appraising and rewarding individual behaviour. In short, performance measurement has profoundly changed societies, organizations and the way we live and work. We can now access incredible quantities of data, display, review and report complex information in real time, and monitor employees and processes in detail. But have all these investments in collecting, analyzing and reporting data helped governments, organizations and people perform better?

Measurement is often associated with the objectivity and neatness of numbers, and performance measurement efforts are typically accompanied by hope, great expectations and promises of change; however, these are then often followed by disbelief, frustration and what appears to be sheer madness. Between the three of us, we have spent over four decades working, consulting, researching and teaching across the wide variety of topics associated with measuring and managing performance, and we are of the belief that performance measurement is first and foremost about behaviours. Our involvement with a large variety of organizations has taught us that performance measurement can be rewarding and frustrating, powerful and amusing, simple at times, but usually extremely difficult.

This book is not another manual on how to design a performance measurement system, or a set of steps on how to introduce the "right" set of performance indicators and the "clearest" dashboard for your organization; the business section of any bookshop is full of such manuals. Instead, this book looks at the consequences and behaviours that plague organizations after they introduce a performance measurement system, and we investigate the reasons why such madness occurs and how these pitfalls could be avoided.

Although performance measurement seemed to promise rational and positive actions, we are today surrounded by dysfunctional and perverse behaviours. Whilst the use of measures seemed to imply that the truth might be found by letting the numbers "speak for themselves", we are now all drowning in a sea of subjective interpretations. Although the introduction of structured reporting systems hoped to encourage openness and transparency in the attainment of social and environmental outcomes, we are currently snowed under by reports compiled mainly for political purposes. And, even though many performance measurement initiatives promised to help managers engage and motivate their people through the use of targets and incentives, our organizations are now rife with cynicism and a lack of commitment.

Of course, the consequences of performance measurement are not all negative, and many organizations have reaped the benefits of introducing and using well-conceived and well-implemented performance measurement systems. However, performance measurement is one of those topics in which the devil is in the detail. It is one thing to design a logical and well-structured system; it is yet another to make it a part of people's everyday lives and ensure that it has a positive impact on performance.

Throughout the chapters of this book we will share with you the various stories and anecdotes that we have accumulated over the years to illustrate the madness that can ensue through the supposedly simple task of measuring performance. Our work and our teaching have taken us across many cultures on all five continents, and we hope that our stories and anecdotes will resonate with you wherever you may be reading this text. In reviewing these stories, what is startling is not just the variety of dysfunctional consequences that performance measurement can generate, but also the scale of the madness – something many of us could never have imagined. However, we do not just describe measurement pitfalls; we also provide practical guidance on how to avoid them. This book is meant to be a light-hearted take on how often and how quickly performance measurement can become absurdly dysfunctional, but it would be remiss of us not to provide indications on how to navigate a way around the common pitfalls. Therefore, this book aims to give you a fun and interesting read, whilst helping you make the task of measuring performance saner, simpler and easier.

Dr Dina Gray
Dr Pietro Micheli
Dr Andrey Pavlov

PART

I

Introduction

I

The Road to Insanity

Performance measurement is everywhere: when we look at companies' financial statements, read reports on average waiting times in hospitals, carry out performance appraisals at work, or look at schools' records when deciding where to educate our children. The practice of collecting, analyzing and reporting information on the performance of individuals, groups, organizations, sectors and nations has been around for a long time – but what difference is it making?

You may be intrigued, enthusiastic or frustrated with measurement, by the behaviours it engenders and the results it leads to. Perhaps you are a proponent of the old adage that "what gets measured gets done" or you may take the alternative view that measurement only leads to dysfunction. Maybe you have used a performance report to make an important decision only to be let down by the result, or perhaps you have been pleasantly surprised when customer performance ratings of restaurants have helped you have an extraordinary dining experience whilst on holiday. Whatever your starting position, this book will not only present real-life stories of madness brought about by measurement, but will also discuss ways to navigate your way around the pitfalls so that you may, once again, use measurement as a means to improve your organization's performance.

In order to set the scene and outline many of the issues covered in this book, we would like to describe a fictional scenario, which is based on the many real events we have observed in practice, about a manager tasked with implementing a strategic performance measurement system and not fully understanding the consequences of such a programme. Let us introduce you to Mike, his hopes, ambitions and challenges.

My name is Mike, and I am a senior manager in a relatively large organization. Today is an important day for me as we are having our annual managers' meeting and I am leading it. The theme for this year's conference is "Performance Excellence". All of the directors and the top managers are here, and we are going to have a series of short presentations on the work undertaken over the past year.

But firstly, let me tell you how all of this has come about. Just over 18 months ago the Board recognized that, as competition was becoming more intense and regulations were becoming ever tighter, we had to improve our performance in all areas of the business. The company therefore commissioned an external firm to carry out a review and they concluded that we were lacking a "comprehensive approach to measuring and managing performance". Essentially, we did not really understand how efficient and productive we were; different units seemed to be run independently from each other; and employees were not clear about the organization's goals.

Shortly after the report was released I was tasked to lead the "Performance Excellence" project, with the aim of introducing a performance measurement and management system throughout the entire organization. It was hoped that the project would completely change the way in which we set and communicate our objectives; how we measure and report performance; and how we appraise and reward people. Today, after a year's work, it is time to check what progress we have made, both in terms of our achievements and in relation to the implementation of the system itself.

At this point in time, before the conference kicks off, I am feeling a little restless, but quietly confident. The lead up to today has been somewhat stressful, and, although I've spoken to most of the people who are attending today, I am not entirely sure what each speaker will say. The organization has always promoted a culture of openness and constructive criticism and I am looking forward to hearing my colleagues' presentations.

I kick off with a short ice-breaker to set the scene, explain what has been done over the past 12 months, and outline future steps. I see a lot of people nodding, which is encouraging as this project has been a priority within the company, and everyone is aware of what is going on. Then I hand over to our CEO. She seems positive about our results, but states that we have to do more as other companies are catching us up and we can't afford to be complacent. Referring to the Performance Excellence project, she says that we have made progress but that she is aware of some "question marks" that we should openly address today. I wonder what those "question marks" could be …?

The CEO concludes and it is now the turn of the Chief Financial Officer. Our financial results appear to be in line with forecast and it seems that we have even had a few unexpected successes. Referring to the Performance Excellence project, he reports that most people tend to regard indicators as relevant or highly relevant, which is music to my ears, but, somewhat unexpectedly, although the number of indicators has increased, the extent to which information is used to make decisions appears unchanged. He continues by saying that despite our immense efforts to provide a balanced view of the company through the introduction of more customer- and process-related indicators, financial indicators are still considered to be the most important ones. This is rather disappointing, even though he concludes by adding that it is just a matter of time before we see more profound changes.

I have to say I feel a bit of relief on hearing his conclusions, but my relief is short lived when, from the floor, one of our regional directors stands up and addresses the executives: "When the Performance Excellence project began we were promised that little effort would be required on our side. Instead, my people have ended up spending a lot of time collecting all sorts of data, yet nobody in headquarters seems to give two hoots about it. I presented our data at the meeting in June which resulted in us spending half an hour arguing over two irrelevant figures, then about the reliability of the data themselves, and we finally took a decision that bore no relation to the data. What was the point of spending so much time collecting and analyzing it?" Before the CFO can utter a response I intervene, pointing out that this should not be happening and that things are changing. From the look on his face I don't seem to have persuaded the regional director, but at least we can now move on to the next presenter.

The Supply Chain Director is up next, and he is renowned in the organization for his obsession with maximizing efficiency. Trained in Six Sigma and brought up on lean thinking, he has been one of the strongest supporters of the Performance Excellence project. His presentation focuses on operational improvements made in warehousing. After a short introduction he goes through a sequence of histograms and graphs reporting the comparative performance of our warehouses. One after the other, in his monotone voice, he presents figures on the number of cases picked per labour hour, inventory accuracy, warehouse order cycle time and finally concludes with a ranking of all of the warehouses.

The league table suddenly wakes everyone up. I was not aware of this ranking, but what harm can it do? If anything, I think to myself, it should spur on a bit of competition among the regional and site directors. However, as he continues on down the list, an ever-increasing hum emanates from the audience. Some people are muttering that it is not clear how the comparisons were made and others question how he calculated the final scores. For me, this is a typical reaction of people who don't want to hear that they are doing worse than others. However, as I consider what he is saying, something starts to bug me: actually not all of the warehouses can be considered to be the same, because we are not using them in the same way. Some of them are inefficient, but that is because they have to handle peak demands; they have to work below capacity for a reason. I make a note that I will have to speak to the Supply Chain Director.

After a short break the conference resumes and the R&D director makes his way to the podium. I should point out that before the Performance Excellence project the organization had unsuccessfully tried to get a grip on this unit, but all attempts to monitor their performance had failed miserably. We had developed a number of measures, such as the number of patents filed, but we had never felt that this was a good indication of the unit's output. What about the R&D workers' productivity? What about forcing them to meet stricter deadlines? Or calculating the unit's financial contribution to the company? I am in no doubt that if we put more effort into more sophisticated measures we will certainly have a more accurate picture and should see an improvement in their performance.

As a bit of background, the R&D director was appointed nine months ago; he was previously in sales, where he achieved great results by introducing individual performance targets and regular, in-depth, performance reviews. Last week when I spoke to him he told me that a few of his R&D people were upset with senior management, although he did not elaborate on why, but he was hoping to resolve the issues very soon. So I am hoping for a critical, but positive presentation. What I get instead is a long list of complaints. He tells everyone that, shortly after he was appointed, he implemented a similar system to the one he had used in the sales department. However, while some of his new team showed their support, the majority of them demonstrated resistance; one could even say sheer defiance. A typical response was "Our performance cannot be measured, we are not sales people!" While he goes through his slides I can't help thinking that people in R&D have had it too good for far too long, and that this research-oriented culture places too low an importance on business performance. To my dismay the presentation ends on a fairly disappointing note with the R&D director suggesting that perhaps the performance measurement system should be designed and implemented differently depending on a unit's tasks and its culture. I am flabbergasted: that's madness, we would end up with dozens of different systems.

It is now the turn of the Sales Director for Western Europe. She says she will be brief: one slide and only a five-minute talk, because "the numbers are the numbers, and they speak for themselves". After a brief preamble, she puts up one chart: her team's improvement is incredible! Sales in her region appear to have doubled over the past year. Can this be right? I look frantically through the draft report I received from Finance two days ago and I can only make out a 5% increase in total company sales over the past three quarters. I don't have a breakdown for each of the geographical areas, but I can't believe we achieved such a positive result in the saturated market that is Western Europe. While the Sales Director performs an act of self-congratulation and is thanking all her team as if they were in the room, I peer at the graph more carefully. It occurs to me that the y axis doesn't start at zero; so, I squint a bit more and I can now see some of the blurred numbers: the real increase is less than 10%! This is really annoying, as we had said that we would be using this forum to openly discuss failures and successes, and then people turn up with lame graphs just to show off. I will have to talk to her too.

The podium is now being prepared for our Chief Operating Officer. At the beginning of this year we made the news for a major fault in one of our products: after several customers reported having the same problem, we were forced to undertake the largest recall in the company's history. Not a happy time. Since we couldn't really blame the suppliers, this hiccup triggered a series of internal arguments between our design and production units. Eventually, the incumbent COO was replaced by his deputy. Before leaving, the old COO wrote an angry letter in which he accused the board of introducing a perverse system of targets and rewards that he labelled "bribes" in his letter, which had completely corrupted the ethics of his team. According to him, people were aiming to achieve tighter deadlines and reduce lead times, but only because they had been promised a short-term financial benefit. This, rather than incompetence or flaws in the processes, was the main reason for the product recall. To me that letter just felt like he was making excuses, but quite a few people at the senior level of the company showed support for his sentiments; so much so that I thought the whole Performance Excellence project was going to be canned. Thankfully, the new COO appears to have opted for a less controversial theme for his presentation and is showing some general trend data, without mentioning performance targets. Phew! There are still strong feelings in the company about what happened and I wouldn't want to have a heated debate right here and now.

The last presentation before my final wrap up is delivered by the CEO of our IT subsidiary. Five years ago she set up an IT firm to provide customized software to companies in our sector. This firm proved so successful that, two years ago, we decided to acquire it. Because of differences in our two histories, tasks and supposed company culture, they have always been given lots of freedom. At the beginning of the Performance Excellence project we discussed whether to introduce elements of the measurement system there, but in the end we decided to run a little experiment instead. In one half of the company things remained the same; in the other half, people capable of achieving "stretch targets" were offered a substantial bonus, up to 30% of their base pay, if they met those targets. In the beginning, a few of the employees seemed unhappy about the introduction of targets; however, since then, sentiment appears to have changed.

Somewhat surprisingly, the presentation starts on a positive note about the Performance Excellence project. Comparative data, recorded in the first two quarters, suggest that during the first six months the people who were striving for a bonus achieved higher levels of performance in terms of both efficiency and quality. This is great; finally we can see that when people are measured, managed and rewarded appropriately they do a better job. However, her second chart shows that this gap has almost reduced to zero over the past six months. It is almost as if people had put in a lot of effort to gain the reward and then just stopped trying. The rest of the presentation spells out the death sentence for my project. It appears that our IT subsidiary is pulling out of the Performance Excellence project because, apparently, quite a few episodes of cheating were found, and customer satisfaction and organizational climate have reached all-time lows.

When finally the last presenter leaves the podium, a deathly hush descends upon the audience. I am not only feeling puzzled, but I am also downright demoralized: I did all I could to get this project off the ground and, after a year, the results are abysmal. But what did we do wrong? Is there any way we can rescue the situation? I reach the microphone, I thank all the previous presenters, and say that we now need time to reflect and think about how to move forward.

Poor old Mike, he has stumbled across the numerous dangers that are inherent in using performance measures and he has discovered that measuring organizational performance is not an easy task. What to measure, how to measure, and perceptions of performance are all key components to avoiding the performance measurement pitfalls described in Mike's story. Throughout the book we will examine and address the issues Mike encountered. For example, Mike discovered that the data that were being collected were not being used for effective decision-making and that the cost of data collection, analysis and reporting was not outweighed by the real benefits achieved. This is a typical case of measurement for measurement's sake. Although Mike knew the business well, he still believed that it would be beneficial to compare R&D to sales, even though they operated in completely different ways. In contexts where measurement is difficult to undertake, we often resort to hoping for A whilst measuring and rewarding B, and this can cause serious damage to employees' motivation and performance. Also, all managers in the company were aware of the emphasis being put on the numbers, especially with respect to their bonuses, and they therefore exhibited classic behaviours to work around the system; even misrepresenting their data to look as though they were overachieving their targets. Dysfunctional behavioural consequences, such as gaming and cheating, that are often determined by misuse of performance targets and rewards, will be investigated in depth throughout the book.

Indeed, there are identifiable reasons why performance measurement fails, and we will review these in the context of the madness that ensues if the consequences of measurement are not considered.

In Chapter 3, "Measurement for Measurement's Sake", we will focus on one of the most common issues associated with performance measurement: the illusion of control that measurement generates and the resulting drive to measure more and more things, in more and more depth. In this chapter we will not only illustrate the negative consequences of this obsession, but we will also give you several ideas on how you can turn performance measurement from a sophisticated technical exercise into an instrument of effective management.

Chapter 4, "All I Need is the Right Measure!", presents problems in designing performance indicators and suggests that, in order for a performance measure to be an effective tool for measurement, it needs to be designed with performance management in mind. The chapter will suggest a number of points that you need to think through if your performance indicators are to become a help rather than a hindrance in the task of improving performance.

In Chapter 5, "Comparing Performance", we present the difficulties of undertaking benchmarking and using league tables in a meaningful way. The learning points will give you tips on determining which data to gather; how to ensure consistency in the collection, analysis and use of performance data; and how to report results without ambiguity.

In Chapter 6, "Target Turmoil", we examine the dysfunctional behaviours caused by an excessive pressure to achieve performance targets. Here we will look at ways to use targets as a means to motivate employees; provide a greater sense of clarity around goals; and, eventually, improve business performance.

In Chapter 7, "Gaming and Cheating", we get to the core of measurement madness and explore the depths that people will sink to in order to play the system in their favour. Whilst you may feel powerless when confronted by such uncontrollable and at times unimaginable behaviours – often targeted at improving reported results rather than underlying performance – we will show you how to take back the initiative, using both technical and cultural ammunition.

In Chapter 8, "Hoping for A Whilst Rewarding B", we describe those situations in which we hope to achieve something, but attain quite the opposite, due to the focus on the wrong measures. At this point we will explore how, by introducing simple systems whose purpose is clear and understood across the organization, you can avoid such unintended consequences.

In Chapter 9, "Failing Rewards and Rewarding Failure", we will navigate the shark-infested waters of financial rewards. Although measures are commonly linked to incentives, the accompanying effects on behaviour are often undesirable, if not downright destructive. Recounting some well-known examples, the chapter will delve into the complex relationship between rewards, measurement and performance. We will also demonstrate how you can use rewards and recognition systems to more positive effects if you have a better understanding of the links between performance measurement and motivation.

Finally, in Chapter 10, "Will Measurement Madness Ever Be Cured?", we will discuss what the future holds for performance measurement and whether cross-organizational measurement systems, or the adoption of "Big Data" analytics have the potential to cure any of the madness described in this book.

As you will see, through reading this book, there is no end to the list of unintended consequences that spring up in organizations due to the application of measurement. We hope that, by emphasizing the outrageous, bizarre and often amusing ways in which people in organizations respond to performance measurement, you will begin to think differently, and challenge some of your own assumptions about the utility of your measurement practices. But let us first look at what "performance" and "measurement" really mean.

2

Performance and Measurement

One of the most puzzling things about performance measurement is that, regardless of the countless negative experiences, as well as a constant stream of similar failures reported in the media, organizations continue to apply the same methods and constantly fall into the same traps. This is because commonly held beliefs about the measurement and management of performance are rarely challenged. However, successful performance measurement is possible. We have worked with numerous organizations that have managed to extract many benefits through the intelligent use of performance measurement. Success stories include businesses gaining an enhanced understanding of their internal and external environment; institutions triggering greater organizational learning; executives having the ability to make more informed decisions; and, ultimately, organizations achieving better financial results and stakeholder satisfaction. However, we are not just relying on our personal experience; a growing body of research evidence has demonstrated that performance measurement systems can be productive and helpful in improving organizational performance.[1]

Yet, more often than not, getting performance measurement right is a difficult task. Therefore, the central question of this whole endeavour is how can organizations use measurement systems as positive drivers of performance and change, whilst mitigating against negative behavioural consequences? Before trying to answer this question, and delving into this minefield of traps and tripwires, we would like to introduce some of the main concepts of performance measurement that will be used throughout the book. Understanding what these terms mean is a fundamental step towards avoiding the main pitfalls of performance measurement.

WHAT IS PERFORMANCE MEASUREMENT?

Different people have different views of what is meant by performance measurement. In this book, we define performance measurement as a formal process, which aims to obtain, analyze, and express information about an aspect of a process, an activity or a person.[2] For example, if we are looking at "customers", we could measure such aspects as satisfaction, loyalty or advocacy. Therefore, we need to be very clear about which aspect we are measuring and formalize the particular elements of the measure. As a minimum we need a definition; we need to specify how we will use the data; and we need to work out how we will derive value. If this is not done, data, on customer loyalty, for example, may be collected in different ways, analyzed in different ways, and interpreted in different ways. It may therefore be of little use, and at worse, misleading.

We have found that most organizations have a performance measurement system in some form or other, be that a scorecard, a dashboard, or a simple framework. Ideally, such systems should consist of three inter-related elements: individual indicators; targets; and a supporting infra-structure that enables data to be acquired, collated, sorted, analyzed, interpreted and disseminated.[3] Importantly, indicators and targets have to be considered not only in terms of how robust they are individually, but also as a collective, because they have to assess the organization as a whole. Hence, the word "system".

However, we are already jumping ahead of ourselves here. There are two distinct elements to performance measurement, the first being *performance* and the second being *measurement*. Let us focus on these two terms individually to see if they can give us any real insight into the nature of performance measurement pitfalls, and help us identify opportunities for improving the practice of performance measurement.

WHAT IS PERFORMANCE?

Before we measure something we must ask whether we understand what it is that we are trying to measure. This question, however, is so obvious that we often take the answer for granted. It turns out though that, in the case of organizational performance, providing the definition of the very object we are trying to measure is far from simple. Moreover, although everyone talks about performance as if it is a common term, they often mean very different things.

If you were to look up the word "performance" in a dictionary, you would come across three relevant definitions.[i] The first refers to the

---

[i] The fourth meaning being "fur trimmings"!

achievement of a *result*, sometimes against a set standard or target. The second refers to the *process* of performing something; in other words, what is being done to achieve the result. If you think about your own organization, it would be interesting to reflect on whether its main performance indicators are related to results, for example return on shareholder value or the number of patients treated; or, to the way in which that output is delivered, such as the productivity of the workforce or the accessibility of the service. The third meaning relates to the act of performing a play, or a piece of music, and how these are *perceived*. When reflecting on an evening at a concert, members of the audience will report, to their friends, whether they thought it was a good or a bad "performance". Does this have any relevance for measurement in an organizational context? Absolutely! The organizational performance that we measure and report on is interpreted by our stakeholders, and it is they who judge whether we have performed well or not.

To illustrate this let us use a sporting analogy. Whatever team you support, be it a soccer team such as Manchester United or Bayern Munich, or a baseball team such as the Boston Red Sox or New York Yankees, you surely want to see your team win. Matches won, drawn or lost is an example of an outcome measure. However, as a fan you will want to see entertaining matches too, as you are also concerned with the way in which your team plays; in other words, you care about the process through which the team achieves its results. However, this is only the view of the supporter. What about if you are a neutral in the crowd? You may only be concerned with seeing an entertaining game. What about the manager of the team? Surely he or she will be focused on the result, as in a lot of cases this will be relevant to their continuing employment. And what about the owners of the team? For them it may be the financial return in terms of attendance, marketing rights and television revenues.

Similarly, let us consider the performance of a public hospital. As taxpayers, we are interested in the efficient use of public money; as patients, we value a responsive and effective service; as members of a patient representative group, we may be interested in openness and the opportunity to collaborate with the hospital; as suppliers, we might want to have clear service level agreements and prompt payment; as employees, we are more likely to identify a good performance with fair wages, security of employment and decent working conditions. So, in all organizations each stakeholder is concerned about that organization's performance, but in different ways. This poses a number of challenges from a performance measurement perspective, because what is being measured is no longer the only factor; who measures and who interprets the data are equally important.

For example, how often have you left a theatre, thinking you have just witnessed a great event, only to overhear another opera buff, on the train home, describe their disappointment at the way the opera had been produced? Likewise, have you ever read the next day's review in the newspaper to wonder if the opera being described is in fact the same as the one you went to see? People have different opinions about the same event and outcome: different stakeholders interpret the performance differently. Even before we get into the measurement and management of performance, we can see how we are dealing with something complex, multifaceted and difficult to pin down.

WHAT IS MEASUREMENT?

In large, diverse organizations, accurately defining what we mean by performance and creating a common view of "true" performance is not just tricky, it is nigh on impossible. To make sense of organizational performance we try to obtain an indication of important processes and activities that represent performance, and then report those results, hoping that everyone will interpret the data in the same way. But, of course, the data reported will only be as good as the measurement undertaken. In a sporting context it is easy to report on the outcome, the number of goals or baskets scored, much like it is easy to report on the number of widgets produced in a factory. However, judging and adequately reporting the *quality* of a sports event, or an opera or a concert is much more difficult, just as measuring employee performance or customer satisfaction or social and environmental performance is in a commercial context.

Consider this scenario. A newly married couple, moving into their first home together, are excited by the prospect of decorating and furnishing their home. They are both keen to paint all of the downstairs rooms, therefore they start by measuring the length, breadth and height of each of the rooms with a standard tape measure. After recording the measurements, they carefully calculate the surface area to cover with paint.

On choosing the colours and paint manufacturer, they elicit the information on the volume of paint required to cover a certain area. Finally, armed with the data, the young couple visit their local do-it-yourself store and purchase the required volume of paint.

Whilst calculating the volume of paint for some home improvement job is a relatively simple task, the same cannot be said about measuring the performance of individuals in an organizational setting. For example, one of our couple, working as a design engineer, is asked by senior management to work out how many projects her team can complete in the next year. The company has calculated standard levels of work a senior engineer and a junior engineer can complete. Counting up the number of engineers at the two levels within her team, our young newlywed makes a number of calculations and confidently predicts an annual output. However, at the end of the year, although her home has been satisfactorily decorated, the number of projects completed has missed her original prediction by 30%. Why is this?

The problem here is, of course, that measures, productivity levels and benchmarks in organizations are not as accurate and precise as those in the physical world. Counting the number of senior engineers does not mean that they all have similar experiences or similar capabilities; after all, they are not tins of paint. These typical problems arise in organizations, because we often start with simple numbers, such as a headcount of engineers, rather than more complex evaluations of their various abilities. Subsequently, we perform some calculations on those data; for example, the annual target for projects to be completed could be determined by multiplying an average rate of performance by the number of senior engineers; and then we take the result as an "objective measure" of performance, rather than as an approximation for it. These simplified approaches ignore individual variation in performance and the intricacies inherent within different projects. Even worse, the very introduction of simple performance measures such as time spent on an activity could negatively affect the behaviours of the engineers, for example encouraging them to focus on easier projects or delaying the completion of projects until the budgeted time is reached. The problem with measurement in organizations is that we assume that the numbers are unassailable, so we confidently make decisions based on those data, and are then surprised by the final result – which is not always a perfectly decorated room.

Since perfect measures of performance do not exist, organizations use *proxies* – indicators that approximate or represent performance in the absence of perfect measures. For instance, higher education institutions use research publications in highly rated journals as a proxy for research excellence or knowledge creation. This solution, however, generates a further problem. Over time, proxies are perceived to represent *true* performance. It is not uncommon for academics to believe that having a long list of publications means that their research is excellent. In other words, the means become ends, and harder to obtain yet critical performance information, such as the quality of the work produced or the impact on teaching, is marginalized, made invisible, with potentially counterproductive effects. One of the most absurd stories in this genre is the use of measurement in the Vietnam War.[4] The US Department of Defense believed that the Vietnam War could be won if the Americans were "winning the hearts and minds of the Vietnamese people". However, given the difficulty of measuring the success of this strategy, the Department of Defense used many proxies, from number of schools built, to number of roads constructed, even to the number of toothbrushes distributed. The results of such measurement gave confidence that the war was being won; the success of such measurement is now consigned to the history books.

Although performance measurement is often linked to tools such as scorecards, dashboards, performance targets, indicators and information systems, it would be naïve to consider the measurement of performance as just a *technical* issue. Indeed, measurement is often used as a way of attempting to bring clarity to complex and confusing situations.[5] From a technical point of view, performance information is gathered, analyzed and communicated to demonstrate results within the organization or to its key stakeholders. For example, if performance information is related to the strategic objectives of the organization, it can be used to show that progress is being made against these objectives. In contrast, performance indicators are often used for *symbolic or political* purposes; in this case, their aim is to increase the relative power of a business unit or department within an organization, or to, apparently, satisfy the demands of external stakeholders. This is evident if we consider how a function within an organization can try to acquire greater legitimacy and power by relying on the measurement of their performance; as one HR director pointed out to us, the sole use of the department's measures was to justify HR's existence to the board! Similarly, as a recent study found, although social and environmental reporting is far more common today than a decade ago, companies that excel at utilizing environmental performance systems may "still emit substantial amounts of pollution. Or, more cynically, they may put in place processes for symbolic purposes but not meaningfully pursue substantial outcomes."[6]

GETTING THE NUMBER OR CHANGING THE BEHAVIOUR?

To date, performance measurement has largely been seen as an exercise in quantifying processes and activities in order to generate data that can be easily analyzed and reported. Whilst this desire to quantify is perfectly logical, as it is important to understand how we are doing, we often overlook the fact that the interpreters of performance data are not necessarily the same in their interests, assumptions and understanding of what has been collected and presented. Also, measurement is not simply a technical undertaking, but it has significant behavioural implications, from extremely positive to incredibly negative.

In this book we will consider the complexity of performance measurement in its entirety – both as an instrument for generating analyzable data and as a powerful driver of behaviour. We believe that you must address both of these aspects before your performance measurement practices can become truly effective. We shall take this step by step and we will start by looking at what happens when the desire to quantify overtakes the basic understanding of what we are trying to achieve.

Performance Measurement

3

Measurement for Measurement's Sake

As you write your end-of-month reports based on data collected through multiple indicators, do you ever stop and consider the reasons for that measurement, or what happens to your reports once they get sent off into what often seems like a black hole? The proliferation of data has exploded in recent years. A recent *Harvard Business Review*[1] article stated that 2.5 exabytes of data are created each day, and more data is sent across the Internet every second than was ever even stored 20 years ago. The likes of Walmart collect more than 2.5 petabytes (2.5 quadrillion bytes) of data every hour from their customers. To get a feel for what these numbers mean, consider that a million seconds is 11.5 days, a billion seconds is 32 years and 2.5 quadrillion seconds is 80 million years!

"Big Data" is certainly changing the way organizations operate, and our capacity to do planning, budgeting and forecasting, as well as the management of our processes and supply chains, has radically improved. However, greater availability of data is also being accompanied by two major challenges: firstly, many managers are now required to develop data-oriented management systems to make sense of the phenomenal amount of data their organizations and their main partners are producing.[2] Secondly, whilst the volume of data that we now have access to is certainly seductive and potentially very useful, it can also be overwhelming, just as in the case of Mike's firm. As the Chief Financial Officer showed during his presentation, although the number of indicators used by the company had increased, the extent to which information was used to make decisions appeared unchanged. Similarly, one of the company's regional directors complained about the amount of effort required for gathering, analyzing and reporting performance information, and the lack of action that followed. So, are we getting better at managing performance or are we simply measuring more?

One of the authors of this book was asked to help with making sense of the performance indicators used by a local authority – one of London's 32 boroughs (districts). Upon arrival, he met with the director of the borough council, who asked him to focus on just one of the 30 divisions that they had, social services, and introduced him to the Divisional Manager. The Divisional Manager, along with his performance analyst, proudly boasted that they had as many as 224 active measures in use, each of which was recorded, tracked, analyzed and reported on. Only a small proportion of this set of measures was mandated by the government; the rest had been introduced by the division itself. The divisional manager stood firm in his defence of the measures as necessary for achieving targets and for demonstrating progress. And remember, this was just one of 30 divisions of the council, so if a similar exercise was repeated in the rest of the divisions, the council would be running 6,720 performance measures!

Measurement is addictive. This property of measurement is at the root of many companies' woes and one of the chief culprits of measurement madness. Tim Ambler, a recently retired scholar at the London Business School, writes, "Important as financial metrics are, they distort reality and provide the illusion of control. Cannabis does much the same."[3] However, as the story above demonstrates, this effect is not restricted to financial metrics. Indeed, any performance indicator, financial or non-financial, forward-looking or lagging, has a strange tendency to capture the fascination of top executives and the attention of managers, gradually taking over much of organizational life. Why is this and how does this happen?

In this chapter we will focus on the various ways in which organizations get carried away with measurement at the expense of their true goals. We will trace the full life cycle of measurement that gets embedded in an organization and, if left unmanaged, slowly takes over organizational time and resources, eventually undermining the very purpose it was designed for. We will also look at the ways in which these issues can be overcome and show that when measurement is kept in check with a set of relatively simple tools, it becomes what it should be: a powerful instrument for managing organizational performance.

MAKING THINGS MEASURABLE

The higher echelons of an Italian police force, feeling that they did not have enough control over, or information about, their officers' movements and coverage on the ground, recently considered the introduction of a set of performance indicators. In itself this sounds like a sane proposition; after all, many police forces around the world, and especially in Europe, have followed a similar path. The first two indicators proposed were "number of kilometres walked per policeman" and "number of kilometres driven per policeman". Given the discussions in the preceding chapters, you should be able to foresee the madness that this could create. One can imagine seeing police cars, driven at high speed to cover the miles, being chased by officers on foot, all for the sake of getting a good score on these measures. But what exactly would these measures tell the higher authorities? Would they be able to compare one regional force with another? Would they be able to set targets for each policeman? And most importantly, what is the performance that they would generate?

As Tim Ambler's quote above suggests, measurement gives us an illusion of control; and control seems to be necessary to achieve goals and move things in the desired direction. Measurement is often seen as a tool that helps reduce the complexity of the world. Organizations, with their uncertainty and confusion, are full of people, patterns and trends; and measurement seems to offer a promise of bringing order, rationality and control into this chaos. In fact, this view of measurement has a long provenance. An enduring quotation about measurement – "what is not measurable, make measurable!" – goes back several centuries to Galileo and his commitment to describe the world in a set of mathematical equations.

Make measurable! The controlling spirit of this quote is almost palpable. Over time, natural science has abandoned this stance and moved a long way to a more modern view of measurement in which it focuses on uncertainty and confidence, rather than on "true values" and "perfect knowledge". However, in the world of management, with its focus on hitting targets and achieving objectives, the illusion of control provided by measurement is almost too tempting to resist. The stories of the Italian police measures and the measures used in academia, reported in the previous chapter, are great examples of what has become known as "tunnel vision"[4] in the performance management field. Tunnel vision occurs when a manager's attention becomes fixated on the easily quantifiable aspects of the work functions he or she has responsibility for. In our examples, this phenomenon is illustrated either by the number of papers published, instead of the generation and dissemination of knowledge, or the distance covered by officers, instead of the effectiveness of police forces' interventions. Tunnel vision is therefore a direct consequence of the addiction to measurement driven by the desire to monitor and control outputs.

MEASURES AND MORE MEASURES

The desire to quantify and the tunnel vision it produces, however, are only the first warning symptoms of an impending addiction to measurement. Even if measures are carefully designed and thought through, the illusion of control provided by the collected data drives managers to measure more and more in order to get more and more data.

Competitive measuring

Working with organizations, we have often had the feeling that the desire to measure has become competitive: measuring more and more seems to be the ultimate goal! As one performance analyst reported to us "We're now a lot further forward than other departments in measuring things and using them to develop the service…Whether we're drowning in them and whether that is taking away from what we want to do, that's an argument as well." Whether excessive information helps or hinders effective performance management is far from clear. Phrases such as "death by data asphyxiation", "analysis paralysis" and "drowning in data while thirsting for information" suggest this may well be the case.

Sticky measures

Why do measures proliferate? In an organization that was, until recently, one of the largest manufacturing companies in the UK, one of the production sites was responsible for a small hut near a river. The machinery in the hut was used to measure the height of the water in the river. For decades the data had been regularly collected, recorded and dutifully reported up the chain of command. A newly appointed manager queried why this data was being collected as it did not appear to have any obvious relevance for the manufacturing operations at the site. The ensuing investigation revealed that the measure had been introduced during World War II, when a bomb, which exploded in the river, had temporarily raised the height of the water to a threatening level. Decades had passed and the water had receded, yet the measure remained present in the performance measurement system and was still unquestioningly tracked and reported.

Another famous story recounts how, in a similar manner, a carpet manufacturer in the North of England recorded "zero" on a daily basis against a measure labelled NART. Once again, nobody really knew what the measure was for, but any new person was told to record zero unless told otherwise. After 60 years somebody discovered that NART stood for Number of Air Raids Today! World War II has a lot to answer for, but who would have thought that the proliferation of meaningless data would be one of them?

The examples above demonstrate that introducing an excessive number of measures is only the start of the problem. The other is that measures tend to stick, unless questioned and revised. As the world changes, so does the environment in which an organization operates. Priorities change, new drivers of performance emerge, and different operating models are employed. It would therefore make sense that the performance measurement system is also revised to reflect these changes. Nonetheless, revisions in performance measurement systems often mean that, although new measures are introduced, old measures are never removed. The resulting complexity makes decision-making harder rather than easier and reduces the overall relevance of the measurement system itself.

Conflicting measures

The issues of obsolescence and the unbounded proliferation of measures, however, can take a more serious turn when a poorly designed or, what is more often the case, a poorly managed performance measurement system allows conflicting measures to operate simultaneously. For a long time, the manufacturing industry relied on automated assembly with its traditional measures of machine utilization and output. Storage and waste disposal were relatively simple and cheap. However, the world has changed, sales volumes have experienced a steady decline, quality and variety have become more important, and, crucially, waste disposal has become more difficult and expensive. However, in a large manufacturing company that we have worked with, we quickly recognized that the performance measurement system had not kept pace with these changes, and the following dialogue was overheard. The manager told the foreman that material being processed in his area was substandard. The foreman, knowing that the only key measure in his line of work was output, responded: "don't worry, we'll make it and Quality Control will scrap it!"

Can the foreman be blamed for his response? The answer is not necessarily clear-cut. On the one hand, you would expect him to understand and care about the way in which his work affects the company. On the other hand, measures provide strong incentives, and following these incentives is often the most rational and predictable course of action. In the example above, the inertia inherent in the performance measurement system produced a situation where the company's strategic goals and shop floor measures were in conflict with each other, leading to the wrong incentives and dysfunctional behaviour. Different functions within an organization often have different priorities – the classic tensions between product design, manufacturing and marketing being a case in point. However, when such functions rely heavily on measures, and the overall consistency of the measurement system is not managed well, the addiction to measurement can generate conflict, which leads to unforeseen consequences.

Losing the link to performance

Regularly, and unfortunately more often than might be expected, organizations can become so fixated on the narrow task of measuring and reporting performance that measures lose their meaning, and no one relies on them for real decision-making. A UK public sector organization, which will remain anonymous, was struggling to make its performance measurement insight actionable. An investigation into why this was happening revealed that the Performance and Quality team was not particularly popular in the organization. At first, it was suspected that this was due to the fact that the team had to ask all the other departments to provide timely and accurate data. However, it was discovered that the team was disliked for completely the opposite reason. Having received the data, the analysts would retreat to their offices only to produce a thick bundle of charts, graphs and spreadsheets, which could rarely be used and were perceived as pointless; so much so that the Performance and Quality team had become known as "the boring department".

More worryingly, sometimes performance measures are introduced without any intention of providing meaningful data for making decisions in the first place. In this case, such indicators are often treated with contempt. One of the authors of this book was recently invited to carry out some work for an Italian government department. His investigation of the measurement records for individual performance revealed a curious formulation of the descriptor for high performance on the individual performance scale. It read: "He/she has demonstrated *excellent* behaviour that has *constantly exceeded* expectations." Although this was not an unusual descriptor on a performance appraisal, the interesting thing about the data was the sheer number of managers and employees that had achieved this gold medal standard (over 90% of the workforce), demonstrating that little regard was being awarded to the appraisal system at all. Such situations are common when measures are imposed on an organization or on organizational units in the form of "best practice" without any participation on the part of the receiver. Therefore, "foreign" metrics often lead to perfunctory measurement whose output is never put to use.

These two examples reflect the all too familiar situation when an initiative, pushed to the extreme, loses its meaning and produces dysfunctional results. Perhaps the Italian government department did not need or was not ready to introduce individual performance measures; perhaps the amount of information generated by the Performance and Quality team was overwhelming; and, perhaps in both situations, the information was not properly integrated into the decision-making processes of the organizations. Although reasons may be manifold, in both cases the addiction to measurement generated multiple measures and a flurry of related activities that had no real impact on performance.

EXCESSIVE RELIANCE ON MEASURES

The dangers of being addicted to measurement do not stop with attempts to quantify the unquantifiable and to introduce and keep as many measures as possible. Performance measures by themselves are simply tools that may or may not be used by managers and staff. However, if your organization has an addiction to measurement, sooner or later people will start relying on measures excessively, and common sense will gradually begin to be replaced by the measures themselves, leading the organization into the eye of the measurement madness hurricane.

Whereas the intelligent use of performance measurement systems breathes life into performance indicators and can deliver the intended benefits to organizations and their stakeholders, excessive reliance on measures can quickly and easily steer measurement off course and can lead to a number of unintended, although often not unpredictable, consequences. Let's have a look at the most common effects of the overreliance on performance measures.

Fixating on measures

An excessive attention to measures and measurement creates something known as "measure fixation".[4] Unlike the concept of tunnel vision discussed earlier, which drives managers to reduce a vague and complex issue to a number of easily quantifiable aspects, measure fixation refers to a situation where people focus on the measure at the expense of the real objectives of the organization. In other words, we try to maximize our performance as measured through a certain indicator, and forget about the very reason for doing so. Have you ever been hung up on, or transferred, by a call centre representative whose allotted response time was up? Or have you ever wondered how crime statistics are calculated?

A good example of measure fixation in police forces relates to an incident that involved one of the authors. Whilst out walking her dog along a public footpath across a pastoral meadow, she was accosted by a local farmer in his old battered Land Rover. The farmer insisted that the dog should be on a lead, although the law states that the dog only needs to be under control. Rather taken aback by the farmer, to placate him the author made her dog come to heel and bent down to put on his lead. As she did so, the farmer drove his vehicle at her, and injury was only avoided because the author and her dog jumped out of the way. Shaken and somewhat perturbed by the incident, she was finally persuaded by neighbours and friends to report the matter to the police. However, the local officer was reluctant to record the incident, as it was the author's word against the farmer's and could therefore not be solved; in the policeman's words, it would "only mess up my figures". You can imagine the author's face when this reason was given for not taking the matter forward.

Another example of measure fixation comes from healthcare. In 2009, in a letter to the *Daily Telegraph*,[i] a group of British doctors, academics and industry leaders criticized the government's approach to palliative care, calling it a "tick-box approach to healthcare". In their letter they drew on their experience with a Liverpool hospice, whose practice of relying on measurement to drive the treatment of patients was proposed to be expanded to cover hospitals and nursing homes in the area. The technique used at the hospice was supposed to alleviate suffering in the final hours of a person's life by using a protocol called the "Liverpool Care Pathway" to assess when a patient is close to dying and, therefore, when feeding and fluid tubes should be removed in order to allow the patient to die peacefully and with dignity. However, as the authors of the letter pointed out, the protocol provided a poor substitute for the actual assessment of the patient's true condition, and yet, as soon as a patient had their tubes removed, the prediction of the patient's death became a self-fulfilling prophecy. Their assessment of this experience was nothing short of damning: "If you tick all the right boxes in the Liverpool Care Pathway, the inevitable outcome of the consequent treatment is death."[5] The authors of the letter went so far as to suggest that the reliance on performance measures had become so excessive that it drove the real objectives of the hospice out of the window, essentially replacing them by a standardized, recorded and reported set of performance metrics, with dire consequences!

If you think that these examples represent one-off occurrences, you could not be further from the truth. Measure fixation is such a powerful consequence of excessive reliance on measures that it can be seen on a national and even international scale. For instance, a recent investigation by the UK's House of Commons revealed that recorded crimes have often been downgraded, and crime victims have routinely been asked not to file complaints – just like in the example above but on a national scale. Raising this issue publicly at the Association of the Chief Police Officers' conference, the Chief Constable for Derbyshire pointed out that there is an overwhelming climate of measure fixation within the service, stating that "The focus for the last 15 years plus has been the statistical performance."[6] The resulting obsession with making the

---

[i] A London based broadsheet newspaper.

numbers, however, undermined the very purpose for which the measures were introduced in the first place.

A year earlier, across the Atlantic, the US Senate Committee on Veterans' Affairs heard the evidence that the Veterans' Affairs mental health care facilities were encouraging their staff to focus on the reported figures rather than on the actual service provided to the patients. For instance, employees in these facilities were asked to minimize the number of cases entered into the system. The *Washington Post* reported one of the former employees testifying that the staff had been directed not to enquire about the patients' general well-being because "we don't want to know or we'll have to treat it". The facilities also manipulated waiting times, eventually enabling the Department of Veterans' Affairs to show that 95% of patients were seen within the prescribed 14-day window, whereas the real figure was less than 50%. In all of these cases, the focus on hitting the measure overtook the underlying task of reducing crime and improving well-being.[7]

Getting desensitized to numbers

The second effect of excessive reliance on measures is that people become desensitized to performance information. Measurement is a process of shifting from a messy reality into the much more ordered and tidier world of numbers. However, in the process of doing so, numbers can erect a wall between us and the real situation. In the wake of the financial crisis of the past decade, the conversations about economic losses, aid and debt seem to have moved from millions to billions and even trillions. But do we really appreciate the magnitude of these changes? In the opening to this chapter we compared scales of magnitude to the number of seconds in terms of years. In our daily work we are bombarded with information such as a 20% downsizing; 15% productivity improvements; halving of product life cycles. Technology companies have "recently predicted that a zettabyte of data will soon be racing about the Internet". What *is* a zettabyte anyway? Apparently, roughly the "equivalent to the information contained in 100 million Libraries of Congress".[2] But what does all this mean in terms of real people, real operations and real time?

When all you see and believe is numbers, it becomes increasingly difficult to decide when to react and intervene. For instance, when the expense line in your budget moves from tens of thousands to hundreds of thousands, is this a cause for alarm? Relying exclusively on numbers makes it nearly impossible to tell. The most obvious course of action is to set aside the numbers and try to understand the underlying causes of these changes. However, the over-reliance on measurement instead drives many managers to design "thresholds" or "colour codes" for numbers, thus adding another layer of abstraction to measurement and keeping these managers firmly desensitized to the meaning of performance information.

Getting lost in performance data

The third consequence of overreliance on measurement is the confusion resulting from the proliferation of performance indicators, coupled with a strong need to report and act on them without understanding why. A major international company that had its own fleet of executive jets struggled to understand properly the work of its pilots. The flight logs simply provided the flight time and duty time. However, the pilots were also involved in many administrative tasks. Some of these were related to flying, for example flight plans or trip preparation; others were purely organizational administrative tasks such as expense reports, operations manual updates, meetings and email. Every month the pilots would be required to produce the record of their daily activity. As with most occupations, there were often multiple tasks per day per pilot, for example completing a four-hour flight and the three hours of associated administrative activities. However, the pilots would only record the dominant task for the day, and flight activity would always take precedence, so very often the administrative work on a flight day would not be captured at all. Likewise, staying at home on a non-flight day, but doing some admin, would not be logged and hence wouldn't show up in the report. This meant that, at the end of the month, the pilot's report could technically show only 12 full days of flying, and yet the pilot would complain of being overworked.

In this case, the focus on the quantifiable aspect of performance was combined with a rigid reporting requirement, and this led to a constant generation of meaningless reports. Therefore, instead of measuring and understanding the actual distribution of the pilots' time, the company consistently collected information that was of no use for managing performance. It would be interesting to see just how much time and effort was spent deciphering and explaining these reports at the pilots' individual performance appraisals!

Another example of getting lost in performance data comes from the defence industry. Building a nuclear submarine is a massive undertaking and one where you can only imagine the focus of effort being put into the quality of the build. When the manufacture of such a vessel comes under the auspices of a very large organization, it is, of course, subject to the same rules and measures applied throughout that organization. Sometimes, however, this can become absurd. An organization we worked with required the filing out of a report on the number of defective submarines that had been returned each week. Not surprisingly, this was always zero!

This example illustrates a different manifestation of the same problem. Whereas the pilots were not measuring what they should, the submarine manufacturers were measuring what they should not. In contrast to the first example, performance reporting in the submarine manufacturing company was accurate, but completely unnecessary! It was caused by the mindless application of a performance measure, which was in turn driven by an excessive reliance on performance metrics.

The proliferation of measures, coupled with the perceived need to monitor and rely on them for decision-making, makes it difficult to keep track of, and utilize, performance information in a meaningful way. If management effort is widely dispersed across everything that can be measured and controlled, the really important signals get lost in a frenzy of measurement activity. Thus, paradoxically, increasing your reliance on measurement renders effective decision-making more, not less, difficult.

Paying the price

Whilst reading these stories, you must have thought that all of this confusion and wasted effort must have a real monetary cost – and, of course, it does. The fourth consequence of an excessive reliance on measurement is the enormous cost to your company. Yet, in an obsessive pursuit of more and better performance indicators, this consequence is often overlooked. In no other area of business would you allow this amount of expenditure without a valid and sensible business case.

However, time and time again organizations fall into the trap of investing money into performance measurement systems without any cost/benefit analysis. Think of these questions: how often has your organization asked itself what return it gets from measuring performance? How often have you tried to calculate the cost of performance measurement? How often have these considerations been taken into account while introducing or expanding your performance measurement system?

Whenever we pose these questions to executives, the room inevitably becomes silent. Very rarely do we see a hand raised, and even then, in most cases, the person tells us that this subject was a matter of a side discussion rather than a formal input into the decision-making process. Yet performance measurement costs money. In the early 2000s, an estimate from the Hackett Group suggested that the average organization with $1 billion of sales was spending 25,000 man days planning and measuring performance. Another study, completed by the Cranfield School of Management, found that large organizations, such as Volvo, believed that up to 20% of management time could be attributed to planning, budgeting and measuring.[8] A study conducted in a single organization by Dr Chris Morgan estimated that as much as 43% of managers' time was spent dealing with performance information and measurement processes. With 350 managers working at the company he researched, and with the average salary of, at the time, £38,000, this translated into an annual cost of approximately £5.7 million; and this figure only represents the monetized cost of management time. Add to this the costs of the IT infrastructure, consultants' fees, accountants' salaries, other opportunity costs, and then, and only then, does the actual cost of performance measurement begin to emerge.[9]

Some of these costs are inevitable for every organization, even when performance measurement is carefully thought through. However, it is important that we estimate the cost of measurement, especially when excessive reliance on performance measures is coupled with an unhealthy level of performance measurement activity. In such circumstances, understanding the return on performance measurement investment becomes of paramount importance. For example, how much does it cost the air fleet division to deal with meaningless pilot reports? How much does it cost the submarine manufacturer to report unnecessary data? And, above all, could these activities have been avoided in the first place if those companies were not addicted to measurement?

Preventing learning and change

Finally, when managers are used to relying on performance measures for everything, from decision-making to rewards and promotion opportunities, change comes at a price and it is often difficult and unwelcome. The decision-making paralysis fuelled by the addiction to measurement can sometimes have devastating consequences. A major European airline, renowned for its attention to detail and unsurpassed customer satisfaction, was struggling to understand why its passenger numbers were dropping dramatically. "We're operationally good and our customers like us, but our financial indicators are mostly in the red", one of the managers reported. Moreover, the company was extremely proficient at measuring performance; they had indicators for both hard and soft assets, including more intangible indicators such as "customer interaction". All possible operational activities and all aspects of customer relationship management were measured to the highest levels of precision. However, what the company failed to recognize was that, with the advent of budget airlines in Europe, the game had changed, and excellent customer interaction, which was charged at a premium, no longer represented a winning strategy. This change had not been reflected in the company's performance measurement system, and the airline remained "committed" to their obsolete set of performance metrics.

LEARNING POINTS

So what have we seen in this chapter? Essentially, measurement can become an addiction, and one of the key factors fuelling this addiction is the illusion of control that measurement seems to provide. This illusion promotes the idea that, if we could only "nail" the elusive drivers of performance with hard metrics, the task of managing performance would become easier and more straightforward. However, we have also seen that there are no shortcuts and that the illusion remains an illusion. Instead of swiftly solving the critical managerial issues and providing a handle on the organizational processes, an addiction to measurement produces a number of undesirable results. Firstly, it drives the desire to quantify, and to quantify everything, including those aspects of the organization that are process-based, intangible, and complex, and that cannot be easily expressed in numbers. Secondly, the addiction to measurement leads to a proliferation of performance indicators, driving managers constantly to introduce new ones whilst retaining the old ones, even when they are obsolete or in conflict with each other. Obsolescence means we end up with measurement for measurement's sake. And finally, when measurement is driven by the desire to control, it forces organizations to rely unreasonably on performance information, leading to an obsessive focus on the indicators, widespread confusion and unaccounted-for costs. So how can these pitfalls be avoided?

We know that when measurement is done thoughtfully and for a purpose, it can be a powerful instrument for improving organizational performance. Therefore, you firstly need to decide on what it is you need to measure to help you improve your organization's performance; then you need to measure accurately and robustly; and finally, you need to manage the organization wisely and not just take the data at face value.

Deciding what to measure

When an addiction to measurement becomes a real dependency, when measures proliferate and stick, and when performance information hinders rather than helps, it is a sign that an organization is operating under the implicit question of: "How can we measure everything?" As the examples in this chapter have demonstrated, however, this is a misleading and insidious question. A better question to ask would be "What do we need to measure?" A well-formulated and exhaustive answer to this question will guide you through the process of selecting the measures that are truly necessary and will ensure that the various measures "talk to each other". Also, it is important to ensure that any possible conflict between measures is prevented or at least known and managed.

An attempt at answering the question of what to measure should begin with clarifying and communicating two things: (1) what constitutes performance for your organization? and (2) what are the drivers of this performance? The most common and most powerful tools for helping you understand what you are trying to achieve and what drives performance are causal maps. These maps exist in different forms. If your strategy and goals are relatively clear, you can use strategy maps.[10] If, on the other hand, you are balancing the demands of multiple stakeholders, each of which has a say in what performance means, success maps may be more appropriate.[11] Irrespective of which type of causal map you choose, it will allow you to see organizational performance as being produced by a causal chain of factors. For instance, as shown in Figure 3.1, let us assume that, for your organization, performance equates to financial results. You may believe that better employee training results in time savings or greater efficiency, which in turn leads to better customer service; customer service is then the driver of higher customer volumes, which lead to higher revenues, and have an impact on profit. If you believe that this represents your chain of performance drivers, then you should focus your performance measurement efforts on these. All other extraneous measures, not relevant to the causal map, may produce superfluous information that will lead you to the detrimental consequences described in this chapter. In fact, if you have mapped out your performance drivers and still have measures that are not on the map, you really need to ask yourself why you are measuring them.

When causal maps are used as part of a performance measurement framework (e.g., Balanced Scorecard or Performance Prism), they will

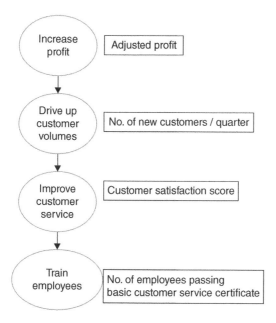

Figure 3.1   Causal map with performance measures.

enable you to identify the interrelationships in the organization and you will therefore be able to spot overlaps and see where there may be a risk of conflicting measures. It is important to remember that as your causal maps are being updated, and as their structure inevitably changes, measures that no longer belong to the map will need to be dropped.

There is, however, one exception to focusing only on a causal map and that is when measures are imposed on your organization by an outside entity, such as a government, a regulator, or maybe even your own global headquarters. In this case your options are threefold: to resist the measures; to treat them separately from your "real" success map whilst still reporting them as required; or to adapt them for your own internal purposes. Whatever path you choose to take, the purpose and the place of these externally imposed measures need to be understood and made explicit.

Designing a robust indicator

One of the key issues we have uncovered in this chapter is the desire to quantify. This issue is driven by the desire to get a handle on the organizational processes and to turn the complexity of organizational performance drivers into something manageable, something that can be acted upon. However, as the examples in this chapter have shown, focusing on what is easily quantifiable at the expense of complexity is not an effective approach to managing performance. Instead of asking how to make things measurable, we should ask "How can we design a robust performance indicator that gives us a good understanding of the situation and enables us to take action?" When the question is framed in this way, the blinkers imposed by the addiction to measurement are removed and you can concentrate on what is truly important, namely, an understanding of what you are trying to measure and how this measure will answer your needs.

Designing an individual performance indicator comes with its own set of issues and can be a source of "measurement madness" in its own right. Therefore, we thought that it warranted a more in-depth discussion and dedicated a separate chapter to it. We will walk you through the intricacies and pitfalls of designing a robust performance indicator in the next chapter. For now, it is sufficient to remember that many issues produced by the desire to quantify can be countered by a thoughtful approach to designing performance indicators.

Managing with measures

When people become fixated on measures, when managers spend a substantial proportion of their time dealing with performance measurement issues, when organizations persistently try to measure the wrong things, and when performance information is so ambiguous and so overwhelming that it gets discarded right away, it usually means that performance measurement efforts are most likely driven by the question "How do we make sure we put all of our measures to use?" The negative consequences of such a take on performance measurement have been discussed in this chapter. A much more relevant and meaningful question should be "How can we manage with measures?"

"Managing with measures" is a term used for a broad approach to measuring and managing organizational performance that recognizes the primacy of performance *management* over performance *measurement*. In other words, managing with measures means that we should know what it is that we are trying to achieve, understand the specific effects and the power of measurement, and employ it accordingly. The addiction to measurement is then replaced with a conscious use of performance indicators aimed at addressing specific needs of the organization. It is, of course, easier said than done, and "managing with measures" relies on getting quite a few things right – targets, compensation and culture in addition to the technical skill of using measurement. We will address these elements in detail in subsequent chapters. The point to remember, however, is that measurement madness usually develops in response to overengineered performance measurement systems and a mindless drive to quantify and measure every aspect of organizational life. Managing with measures is that "soft component", which ensures that measurement is carried out for a purpose and that the task of getting better at measurement never overtakes the overarching goal of improving organizational performance.

AND FINALLY...

Using performance measurement effectively is a tricky thing: understanding what to measure, designing robust indicators and keeping the number of indicators down requires constant attention and willingness to learn. Drop this for a moment, and the addictive pull of measurement can suck you right back into the whirlpool of measurement madness. Several years ago, at the height of the worldwide performance measurement craze, we delivered a seminar to a group of senior managers in the public sector. During the seminar, one of the delegates shared with us that he had as many as 160 measures to report. "This must be extremely stressful!" one of us empathized. "On the contrary!" the manager retorted. "It's great! At any given moment, at least one of them is going up!"

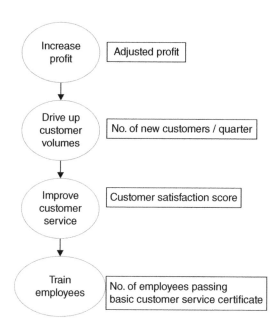

All I Need is the Right Measure!

Although recent advances in automobile manufacturing have delivered ever-increasing safety for drivers and passengers, road traffic accidents continue to act as a threat to life and limb. By their very nature, road incidents are highly visible and attract attention both on the part of the public as well as national and international governments. Organizations such as the World Health Organization and the International Transport Forum routinely publish road accident reports, comparing injuries and fatalities across different countries. One would imagine that a road accident fatality indicator would be easy to design, and the compilation of comparative statistics would be fairly straightforward. However, nothing in the world of measurement is easy or straightforward!

So how do countries measure and record road accident fatalities? It turns out that the answer depends on where you measure it, how you measure it, whom you ask, where the data comes from and whether there are any incentives to show a particular level of performance. Does that sound familiar?

To begin with, different countries have different definitions of what constitutes a road traffic fatality. According to the most common definition, which is adopted by the International Road Traffic and Accident Database (IRTAD), a road traffic fatality is recorded if a person involved in an accident dies within 30 days of the incident. This is a relatively simple definition, which, according to IRTAD, is based on substantial medical research. At the time of writing this book, however, the IRTAD recording system has been adopted by only 29 countries. These include the majority of the countries in the European Union as well as the United States, Canada, Australia, New Zealand, South Korea and Japan. In the rest of the world, however, the same indicator is defined differently, and the formula ranges from "death within 24 hours of the crash" in Vietnam to "seven hours" in Russia and to an incredible "one year from the crash" in Moldova.

It gets worse! Even if a definition could be standardized, calculating the value of the indicator correctly would require a consistent approach to recording and reporting the data. This, however, quickly gets difficult. In Mexico, for instance, road fatalities are recorded by two different law enforcement bodies, depending on whether the accident occurred in a city or a suburban area, or on a federal road. Calculating the final number therefore depends not only on having a clear definition, but also on having comparable procedures to ensure the continuous and consistent data sharing between two organizations. If you think that this problem is peculiar to Mexico and a limited number of other countries, remember that whenever the definition allows for anything longer than "death at the scene of an accident", calculating the indicator correctly requires constant and consistent synchronization of data between the police, who record the accident itself, and the healthcare system, which records whether the injured person passed away within the time period prescribed by the definition of the indicator. This is not a simple task even for countries with established systems for keeping public records.

And lastly, even if the definition of the indicator can be nailed and the infrastructure for recording and reporting the data can be designed and implemented – a big if! – there are a few "softer" issues to consider. Firstly, adopting a definition with a wider time window is bound to inflate the number of deaths whilst at the same time artificially reduce the number of injuries. As changing the indicator is nothing more than a policy decision, it is open to political expediency. Secondly, recording the data does not mean that the numbers will then be collated and reviewed with the same frequency, or even at all. And finally, the real question is whether this indicator will have an impact on decisions and policy making or whether it will just remain an expensive measurement exercise.[1]

In this chapter, we take a closer look at performance indicators and show that although a single performance indicator may well provide you with the information and knowledge that you need to understand and improve the performance of your organization, it also holds the power to thwart your best intentions. As we are often asked by companies to provide a set of KPIs (key performance indicators) for, say, a marketing team or for an HR department, we hope to demonstrate here that an indicator is not just a KPI that you can pull off a shelf. Our aim is to help you consider the nuances of designing and implementing performance indicators in a way that will allow you to steer clear of performance measurement pitfalls. We begin by looking at what factors should be considered when designing and critiquing an indicator and we show what happens when these factors are overlooked or neglected.

HOW DIFFICULT CAN THIS BE?

In the business sections of many bookshops you are likely to find thick volumes listing hundreds of performance indicators. The unspoken promise of these catalogues is that you can take a standard indicator, transfer it safely into your own environment and start reaping the benefits immediately. On the one hand, these types of publications are useful as it is important to see what other organizations have done; there may be some relatively standard indicators that could be used for benchmarking; and you could use an existing list of indicators to get ideas for what to do in your own organization. On the other hand, if you think that these indicators are "ready to be implemented", you may quickly fall down the first measurement hole. As we discussed in the previous chapter, your measures should be aligned to your strategy and therefore your indicators need to be designed to your own specifications. Imposing measures on people, who may or may not understand them, is not the ideal way to get them embedded in the day-to-day work of your organization.

We have found that it is almost always better to go through the pain of designing your own performance indicators from scratch than to implant standard metrics into your organization, then crossing your fingers and hoping that they will take root and do what you expect. Here we describe the critical elements of a structured process for designing an indicator and we discuss why it is important to get the elements right.[2] Even if, after this warning, you do decide to go with a standardized indicator lifted from a catalogue, you may wish to critique the indicator using this same process.

What's in a name?

The first questions to ask is whether your indicator is named appropriately and whether everyone in your organization can relate to it. The best indicators have short and descriptive titles that leave little room for misunderstanding what they are designed to do. Consider this renowned example.

The 1990s saw the first true revolution in the personal computing industry. As the market was quickly becoming customer driven and moving towards mass customization spearheaded by the likes of Dell, traditional manufacturers of PCs quickly realized that their inventory was their biggest liability. No longer could they ship large volumes of stock to traditional retail outlets and wait for the customers to come and purchase their PCs. Therefore, understanding how inventory management affected the cost base became a crucial factor in ensuring long-term profitability. Responding to this need, Hewlett-Packard (HP) introduced a composite performance indicator; they firstly identified every way in which inventory-related decisions were made that could affect the company's costs; these included manufacturing, sales, rebates, and product rollouts to name but a few. Then HP integrated all of these factors into a single metric. It was a highly sophisticated indicator, which required collaboration not only across departments within HP and but also with the company's suppliers and buyers. The indicator was called "IDC – The Inventory-Driven Cost". Despite the complexity behind it, the title of the indicator was short, understandable, free of jargon and it summarized exactly what the indicator was meant to reflect.[3]

Many good examples of appropriately named indicators can be found in finance and accounting, simply because these areas have established standards and a consistent language. In marketing and strategy, on the other hand, there is often a tendency to get carried away with fashionable terms such as "customer delight" or "learning organization", which can mean different things to different people. If you are implementing an indicator, remember that anyone for whom this indicator is relevant should be able to get a grasp of what it means without delving into the small print.

Knowing the purpose

During a recent research project one of our authors came across an entrepreneurial software company that reacted quickly to the market and was establishing a reputation for the quality of its work. Being a typical dot-com, the employees loved coming to work, it was a great environment and many of the developers spent more time at their desk than they did at home. The HR department was keen to establish its credibility within such an environment and decided to commission some work to create a tool to report on absence from work. After a number of months, and a substantial cost, the HR team gathered the data, analyzed the numbers and presented their findings to the board. The directors were not amazed by the findings, as it told them something that they already knew – that there was no problem with sickness and absence in the company.

Unfortunately, the story above is not rare. Very often we see indicators being introduced, or kept, for no other reason than the data for them is readily available, the procedures are clear, it is easy to track and report and current performance is satisfactory. However, as we discussed in the previous chapter, performance measurement is an expensive activity, and therefore knowing the purpose of each indicator is absolutely critical. The key question to ask yourself is "Why are we measuring this item?" and if a satisfactory business reason cannot be given it would be prudent to stop at this point.

It is, of course, possible that you may need to employ indicators that are not directly relevant to your business. For example, in the public sector, many performance indicators are mandated by the government, and local bodies are legally required to implement, track and report on particular aspects of performance. Likewise, in the private sector, credit rating agencies such as Standard & Poor's may ask you to track a particular indicator so that the performance of your company can be compared to that of your competitors. Regardless of this, however, being clear about what purpose each of your indicators serves helps you avoid many of the performance measurement pitfalls described in this book.

Poor relations

During World War II, due to the desperate shortage of fuel, many companies in the UK encouraged their employees to cycle to work. As part of this initiative, these same companies kept a record of the number of people arriving on bicycles. When introduced, the indicator was clearly related to the goals of saving money and helping the nation. However, as we saw in the previous chapter, performance indicators have a tendency to stick, and many companies continued keeping the record and reporting the indicator long after the end of the war. As the measure was no longer related to an organizational objective, it had lost its meaning, and the information stored was not used for any purpose. Although the significance of this indicator has once again become relevant, for objective reasons, such as measuring the carbon footprint of a company or tracking the benefits of a healthy lifestyle, it is not good practice to keep an indicator just in case it becomes useful at a later date!

In order to stop the proliferation of unnecessary indicators it is therefore useful to understand what organizational objective the measure relates to. If a relationship cannot be forged then once again the utility of that indicator should be questioned.

As well as clarifying the link to an organization's goals and objectives, much measurement madness can be prevented by asking what other performance measures the indicator relates to. As you will see in the coming chapters, conflicting measures are a constant source of frustration, cost, and gaming behaviours. That is why, as performance indicators are designed and rolled out, it is vitally important that the people who will be using them understand what these indicators relate to, both in terms of the overall organizational objectives and in terms of other performance indicators.

It's in the formula

Automating performance measurement and reporting often holds the promise of lower costs and higher efficiency. One of the government agencies in Russia, with whom we have worked recently, introduced electronic paperwork, not only to reduce the amount of paper used but also to effectively track the work of the employees. One of the metrics the agency introduced for travel clerks was entitled "The number of documents processed". In this system the manager could simply call up an employee's record and see what documents had been worked through and closed, how many documents had been completed and by when. However, as is often the case, the managers would not normally have time to analyze the electronic reports in depth, and so they would simply review the bar chart that reflected the number of documents processed.

An interesting, albeit not altogether surprising, situation developed. When travel clerks created documentation packages for group business trips, they would create separate documents for each person travelling instead of preparing one document for the entire delegation. As a result, their end-of-week report would show serious effort and high output. When challenged about this behaviour, the travel clerks countered that they had done nothing wrong, in fact they had done exactly what they believed the managers expected of them from the title of the measure.

This problem illustrates that having a clear and concise title for the indicator is often not enough, it is equally important to specify the formula to show how the indicator will be calculated. All too often managers believe that everyone will automatically use an indicator in a consistent manner. In the example above, it is almost certain that the clerks knew that the high performance being reported was an illusion and that they were simply exploiting a poorly defined formula. In this case a better formula would specify exactly what kind of documents count towards the measure, what a "processed document" means and when the count begins and ends.

This is a relatively simple example, but a word of warning about formulae, especially where you have more than one factor in an equation. Consider one of the most commonly used financial formula, that of profit. Profit is normally calculated as revenue minus cost, but, of course, profit can be artificially inflated by cutting your costs to a minimum. However, do not swap simplicity for complexity. In our experience, when indicators have even more sophisticated formulae it is rarely justified by the nature of what is being measured. Be aware that when a formula becomes overcomplicated, however good the intentions were in the first place, it is often the case that these indicators are pushed aside and never become part of the decision-making process. Therefore, it is extremely important to work out tight rules for calculating "performance" and to make sure that people understand exactly what is being measured, how it is being measured and why.

Frequency

In early 2013, the entire food supply chain in Europe was shocked by the revelation that beef products on many supermarket shelves actually contained traces of horse meat and pork. The news quickly gained public attention, and the media promptly dubbed the unravelling meat contamination scandal as "Horsegate". Although the adulterated products posed no threat to public health, the scandal raised serious questions about the transparency of the food supply chain across Europe and the traceability of the origins of the many products that we consume.

The Horsegate scandal started in late 2012 when the Food Safety Authority of Ireland (FSAI) conducted a number of tests that indicated the presence of horse DNA in products that were marketed as beef. Horse meat was found in 10 out of 27 "beef" burgers that the agency tested under their "meat authenticity survey",[4] which was carried out in conjunction with its *annual* monitoring programme; so these tests were conducted at most once a year. Our question for you is: how often do you think these tests should have been conducted? Weekly? Biweekly? Monthly? What frequency of measurement would you choose for the "meat authenticity" indicator?

It is easy to criticize the policy of the FSAI, but if there are no risks to public health and safety, an annual check of food authenticity may be all that is required. After all, measurement is an expensive activity and the more frequently you measure the more costly it becomes. However, other considerations were at play here, including the truthfulness of advertising, the respect for consumer choice and the reputation of the retailers. While an annual check of this kind may be acceptable for a government agency whose primary concern is public health, the frequency may well be too low for a supermarket whose reputation depends on public trust.

While the food industry is still debating the appropriate frequency of measuring food authenticity, our point here is that a performance indicator is incomplete unless you consider how often the measurement should be taken. Designing an indicator with a robust formula is important but is not sufficient. Deciding on the frequency of measurement is one of the major decisions that you need to take in order to ensure that an indicator serves you well.

Finally, it is important to remember that there is a difference between the frequency of measurement and the frequency of review to support timely decision-making. For many indicators, measurement is automatic, such as the tracking of business mileage or travel expenses on a corporate credit card. However, how frequently the numbers are collated and reviewed is a management decision. The frequency of measurement and reporting are often those quiet considerations behind which many questionable practices can hide.

Where does the data come from?

Many supermarket chains now offer a home delivery service. Instead of spending hours pushing the trolley along endless aisles and then standing with it in similarly endless checkout queues, customers can now spend a few minutes at their computers and have the grocery van pull onto their driveway within a couple of hours. One of the key features of this service is the offer of a one-hour time slot, which the customer picks and during which the delivery will be made. It is such a powerful differentiating feature that several supermarket chains offer their customers compensation if their delivery driver misses the agreed delivery slot. "On time delivery" is then a crucial performance indicator for both the company and the customer. But where does the data come from?

Very recently, one of the authors of this book found himself receiving a delivery from one of the UK's largest supermarkets. The booked delivery slot was 20:00–21:00, but the actual delivery time was 21:02. Knowing that the drivers usually ask the customer to record the delivery time next to their signature on the delivery sheet, our author asked:

"Is there something I need to write here?"

"Oh, just your signature at the bottom, and you'll be fine", replied the driver waving his hand towards the bottom, of the sheet.

"Anything else?"

"No", he asserted, "that's fine. I'll take care of the rest."

Not wanting to give the driver any additional hassle on a wet winter's night, the author returned the signed paper to him.

Now, let us think about what this situation means for the performance information that the company tracks. Perhaps the driver later recorded the correct delivery time, perhaps not. What is important is that the way the indicator and the support infrastructure were designed allowed the driver, and admittedly the customer, discretion over the result of the measure. This level of discretion could lead to performance pitfalls such as gaming by the driver, data manipulation and so on.

These days many large organizations employ Enterprise Resource Planning (ERP) systems, from vendors such as SAP, Oracle or Microsoft, to manage the large quantities of data that they hold and to produce reports on various aspects of the organization. However, as the example above demonstrates, it is extremely important to consider how the data is collected and entered into the ERP system. In addition, if your ERP system pools data from different databases with different standards, as in the case of recording road accidents in the opening example to this chapter, validation of the outputs will be essential. Data entry is therefore one of the first cracks through which measurement madness can enter your organization, and, if left undetected, it will simply be amplified by the subsequent performance measurement and management procedures. Of course, you may consciously choose to allow discretion in data entry, for instance when measuring complex things, but the fact remains that thinking about where the data comes from must be an integral part of your performance indicator design.

What will you do with the results?

Similarly to what happens in most countries, ministries in Italy have both political and administrative leadership. The elected politicians assume the overall control of the ministry and decide on the general policy, whilst civil servants are tasked with implementing the policy and managing the day-to-day operations of the ministry. Although the management hierarchy within ministries is headed by senior civil servants, the highest position belongs to the minister. Therefore, in terms of performance management, it is the ministers who evaluate the performance of civil servants. That, at least, is the theory. In his appointment to an Italian government agency working on performance measurement and management across the country, one of the authors of this book discovered, in one of the ministries, a document that outlined the performance evaluation procedures. The document stated that, although the authority of the elected minister was acknowledged, the ministry's "top management, because of its onerous and complex tasks, *may* be evaluated by the political leadership, whereas the rest of the organization *must* be evaluated". So, whatever effort and care might have gone into the development of performance indicators for senior civil servants, the appraisal process gave the top management an effective escape route.

The example above illustrates the idea that performance indicators by themselves will never give you the solution you want, no matter where they came from, how precise the formula is and how much time and effort you spent reviewing them and adjusting them to your context. Although it may sound trite, an indicator is only useful when it is used. Therefore, unless your indicators come with a clear set of answers about who conducts the measurement, who acts on the results of this measurement and what exactly they are expected to do, these indicators risk becoming tools for information hoarding, power games and many other aspects of measurement madness. However, working out the answers to these questions will allow you to connect an indicator with the way your organization operates. By doing so, you will begin to bridge the gap between performance measurement and performance management. As you will see in the coming chapters, this is the only sure way to get value from performance measurement whilst maintaining your sanity.

What the discussion above demonstrates is that although performance indicators are often hailed as the solution to performance-related problems, they very rarely are. "We need a set of KPIs" is often a response that fails to recognize two major issues. Firstly, finding or designing a robust indicator is difficult. Every aspect of performance indicator design, from the way it is named to the way it is calculated, has the potential to throw you off course and subvert any good intentions you may have had when introducing measurement into your organization. Secondly, by themselves indicators are inert, they are simply tools that may or may not deliver value depending on whether and how they are used. Therefore, in order to be able to trust your performance measurement system you need to consider all of the aspects of performance indicator design described in this chapter and summarized in Table 4.1.

HOW STRONG ARE YOUR INDICATORS?

The first half of this chapter has challenged the common view that a good indicator is all that's required to deal with performance-related issues. Introducing a new performance indicator is indeed more nuanced and more challenging that it may seem at first sight. However, it may be the case that you do not even have the luxury of implementing new and robust indicators. You may well find yourself in a situation where you are handed a set of indicators and expected to make the best of it. The second part of this chapter aims to help with such a situation. Using the Ten Tests of a Good Measure,[5] we will show you how to evaluate the robustness of indicators, new and old, and help you anticipate any issues with their implementation.

Table 4.1 The aspects of performance indicator design.

Element	Why is it important?
Title	To avoid misunderstandings over what the indicator actually measures.
Purpose	To understand why the indicator was introduced and to check its relevance. Prevents the introduction of unnecessary indicators.
Relates to	To establish explicitly which business objective the indicator serves and which other indicators it relates to. Prevents the introduction of irrelevant indicators, creates synergies and helps to avoid conflicts with existing indicators.
Formula	To guarantee consistency in measurement and avoid gaming behaviour.
Frequency	To ensure timely information, whilst keeping costs down.
Who measures? and Where does the data come from?	To make sure data is robust and trustworthy.
Who acts? and What will they do?	To guarantee that performance indicators are utilized and that performance information is acted upon.

Is the indicator measuring what it is meant to measure?

Skiing is a pleasurable pastime, enjoyed by many. Even the most casual skiers like to test themselves by tackling different and more challenging slopes as their skill progresses. Ski slopes in Europe are graded, in terms of difficulty, from *green* through to *blue*, to *red* and finally *black*. The US system is slightly different, as US resorts use a grading system that ranges from *green*, to *blue*, to *black*, to *double black diamond*. We don't think this is because American slopes are so much more difficult; it is just that European *red* is replaced by a *black diamond*. In some resorts, such as Breckenridge in Colorado, the grading isn't quite as simple, and, because they don't use *red*, they define some slopes as *blue/black*.

Having different scales representing the same difficulty of slopes creates confusion. However, this doesn't change the challenges that the recreational skier faces. There are real safety reasons for grading slopes, as we all know the level of our ability, and can judge whether we are a *red* or a *black* slope skier. However, there is also some kudos in the bar in the evening, reporting on the grade of slope you have skied during the day. What doesn't usually change though is the mountain itself: if you return to a resort, you will know where the easy or more difficult slopes lie. Imagine the surprise one of our authors felt when it was found that a *blue/black* slope had been upgraded to *black* with no perceived difference to the steepness of the slope or to the difficulty of the terrain! Using this new categorization, does it now mean that the performance of the skier has improved? Although there are now more people being able to boast that they have skied a *black* run, where is the validity in all this? Are these grading processes really measuring what they are supposed to measure, or are they just making people feel good?

As the example above suggests, the first test of an indicator is the validity test. In the commercial world you should avoid changing the measure, or related codes, in order to demonstrate that performance has improved. Consider what you are trying to measure and check that the indicator you are using provides a good reflection of it.

Although this may sound obvious, a large number of indicators we see in our practice fail this test. For example, a consulting firm we worked with used "headcount" as a measure for the organizational knowledge that the firm held. Although headcount is relatively easy to calculate, as you can imagine, it offers a very poor approximation of the knowledge the organization has. Very similar to this is the use of "R&D spending" as a measure of innovativeness. Another very common example is using "repeat purchases" as a measure of customer loyalty. While this makes sense for an organization operating in a highly competitive market where customers have a lot of choice, it is much less meaningful for a company that is the only provider of a particular product or service and whose customers are effectively "locked in". So, when you evaluate your indicators, check their validity by asking whether they really are measuring what they claim to be measuring.

Is the indicator only measuring what it is meant to measure?

Another important point to consider when designing or reviewing a performance indicator relates to its focus. Unnecessarily complex indicators will often not only measure what they intend to measure, but also incorporate interference from other aspects of the environment. Typical examples of this are customer satisfaction surveys, in which several, partly overlapping, aspects are captured: for instance, customer advocacy indicators often mix up elements of "willingness to recommend", "net promoter scores" and other related but separate indicators. Survey results in this case would capture many things, but only a few of them would be connected to the actual satisfaction of customers with the company's services or products. Complex measures such as brand identity and recognition often have the same issues.

Customer satisfaction surveys often fail the focus test because they consider various aspects that are not strictly related to the issue under consideration. Other indicators can fail this same test for the opposite reason: they measure only part of what they are supposed to measure. For example, several logistics companies use "truck fill" as a measure of environmental sustainability, as reducing "empty mileage" is a benefit to the environment. However, clearly this indicator does not fully capture the environmental impact of a company's operations, and it is even more problematic when used for benchmarking purposes as it is strongly influenced by different company strategies. For example, you may compete on timeliness of deliveries, in which case you may not be able to wait until the truck is fully loaded. Equally, there are other factors that play a major role in the environmental impact of a firm that may not be captured by "truck fill", for example the age of the fleet, speed of driving, etc.

Is the indicator definitely the right indicator?

Many families in the UK receive a state payment called Child Benefit for any children under the age of 16, or under 20 if that child is still in full-time education or training. Only one parent can claim the benefit, and for historical reasons this has normally been paid to the mother. Until recently, this was a universal benefit, meaning that it was neither taxed nor means tested. Following the banking crisis in 2007 and a period of austerity declared by the Chancellor of the Exchequer,[i] the payments for Child Benefit came under close scrutiny. The UK government decided that the best measure of whether somebody deserved to receive this benefit would be if either one of the parents exceeded the higher rate tax bracket; at the time, the threshold was £43,875.

---

[i] The UK's finance minister.

This was an easy threshold to track, and the stopping of benefits could be simply automated. On the face of it, this appeared to be a fair measure. However, as soon as it was introduced, families were up in arms, as the new system hit the families where one parent elected to stay at home and look after the children and the other parent earned just over the rate, say, £44k. Such a family would then lose the benefit. However, for a working family, where both parents earned just under the threshold, the household could bring in £86k and still keep the benefit. So was the "level of tax paid by one parent" definitely the right indicator to use for the new policy?

The UK government provides us, alas, with another example of madness in this category. In 2011, the government decided that it would be fairer if everyone paid for their own higher education fees and that institutions set the fees for each course they delivered. The aim was to stimulate market forces whereby the more renowned universities would be able to charge a higher fee than those with a less credible reputation. However, with an eye on the voting public, the government did not want to price out potential students from poorer backgrounds and therefore set a cap on fees of £9,000 per year. While this policy has a certain logic, university education is not a commodity that can be sold to the lowest bidder. As price would send a signal to the public in relation to the quality of the course, no institution wished to be seen as providing a lower quality of education. Therefore, virtually all courses at all universities were priced at £9,000.

Very often, performance indicators are selected according to the "good enough" criterion: we are not searching for the best possible indicator, but for one that is good enough for our purposes. However, as you can see from the examples above, it is extremely important to pause and think about whether the indicator being used is actually relevant to the context and to the goals that your organization is trying to achieve.

Is the indicator consistent regardless of who measures and when?

In September 1999, NASA reported that it had lost a $125 million Mars orbiter. After a 286-day journey, the Mars probe had fired up to push the craft into an orbit around the planet. However, the craft had then come too close to the surface, within 36 miles of the planet, and could not function properly. While all space explorations are prone to mishap, one of the reasons for this particular failure was down to an inconsistency of measurement. A Lockheed Martin engineering team based in the UK unfortunately used the imperial units of measurement rather than the metric units used by their NASA counterparts.[6] In their communications, both teams were talking about speed, distance, acceleration and so on, but they failed to realize that they were measuring this in different ways. Now, if the world's top scientists and engineers can't get the consistency of their measurement correct, what hope is there for the rest of us?

Just as the result may be affected by who takes the measurement, the timing of measurement can also play a role. For instance, for many parcel delivery companies, delivery time is a highly seasonal indicator. Delivery times in the northern hemisphere will be shorter in August, when people are on holidays, the roads are clear and the volumes are low, than around Christmas, when the road conditions are poor and the volume of deliveries shoots through the roof.

As you evaluate your performance indicators, remember that the same measure must give you the same result regardless of who takes the measurement and when and where it is taken. When this is impossible, you must complement your measure with adjustment procedures in order to prevent distortion from creeping in.

Can the data be readily communicated and easily understood?

One of the authors recently carried out some work with a company that was operating in three very different geographical areas. Each region was relatively autonomous and although they shared the same strategic goals, they were free to decide which performance indicators to use. This appeared to make sense, at least to some extent. For example, one region would measure production processes more closely as most of the plants were located there. However, although customer satisfaction was regarded as a clear area of interest for all regions, the devolvement of measurement practices meant that one region would measure customer satisfaction through brand loyalty and brand preference; another used two different customer satisfaction scores (named "competitive" and "best in class"); and the third had developed a customer satisfaction index of its own. When the performance management team, which sat in the corporate office, had to combine measurement results for the overall company customer satisfaction score, it proved to be a nightmare. Firstly, different formulae were used. Secondly, the performance management team had to wait for all regions to upload their information onto the corporate system, and then they had to rework all data into some kind of a summary, which was achieved through a composite and quite obscure satisfaction index. The result was that the only available information at the quarterly board meetings was a quarter out of date and was presented as a numerical score (e.g., 3.58) with no real explanation of what it meant. This was clearly a disappointing outcome for such an important area.

Communicating performance information should be as neutral, clear and effective as possible. Accessible data is easy to conceptualize, but the myriad of ways in which data can be reported, the biases this often leads to, and the misinterpretation that this engenders, means that what started out as a simple idea can turn into impenetrable numbers and confusing text.

Is any ambiguity possible in the interpretation of the results?

Measuring the performance of a health system, in this case the UK's National Health System (NHS), is not an easy task. Health outcomes, social outcomes, quality of life, social equality, as well as financial measures, should all be included to provide a balanced and comprehensive view. Clearly, using the financial costs of outputs as a proxy for such complex constructs is inappropriate. Even if outputs could be defined and measured as a single number, it would be nonsensical to express it as a ratio of financial input measures. A report published by the UK Office for National Statistics[7] recognized this and was littered with alerts urging restraint in the interpretation of the results:

> These (productivity) estimates should be interpreted with care. The output figures are based on a subset of activities in the English NHS and do not include changes in the quality of NHS output. The inputs figures are also not ideal, as direct quantity measures would be preferred, and the existing method involving measurement of current price expenditure and using indices to deflate to quantity measures for England only needs improvement. (p. 52)

However, despite all of these caveats, the Office for National Statistics then pursued the very financial cost approach it criticized: to simplify the analysis, purely financial elements were included in the productivity ratio produced by the report. Therefore the main conclusion of the report was that NHS inputs had grown by between 32% and 39% whilst output had risen by only 28%, representing a substantial decrease in efficiency. Even this oversimplified analysis faces significant challenge, as calculating reasonable estimates for the financial inputs and outputs of the NHS is also incredibly complicated. Despite all the methodological caveats and the complexity involved, these raw numbers were seized upon and publicized by both the media and politicians, leading to such headlines as "The NHS is 'wasteful and inefficient' ".[8]

As this example shows, if the conclusion is isolated from its context, the clarity of the message is blurred and gives misleading views. Compromising on clarity and structure during the measurement process is often the first step towards measurement madness. Also, low quality data and poor analysis will invariably be compounded by the biased interpretations of individuals being presented with data out of context. Finally, the example above is a perfect illustration of the fact that even financial figures, which are often welcomed as the clearest and least ambiguous, are open to misinterpretation and therefore require a great deal of care.

Can and will the data be acted upon?

One of the most common complaints we hear by those who have to collect and report data is that they never know whether or not the data is useful or is even considered by those who request the reports. We have encountered managers who have told us that they have stopped spending time and effort collecting data and writing extensive reports, initially because they were interested to see if anyone would notice, and then because nobody ever complained that the reports were missing. Given the amount of time it takes to collect and report on an indicator, which is a real expense to the organization, it is essential that all data is reviewed and action taken. Unfortunately, many organizations only react when the data indicates bad news. The best design of an indicator should also specify what action should be taken when the data signals good news.

If managers or those responsible for collecting and reporting data do not believe that anything happens with the data recorded by the indicator, then the care taken over the quality of the data being reported will dwindle.

In a high reliability organization responsible for nuclear safety we witnessed a strategy review where the long-term (125 years) plan was being discussed. Prior to this meeting the operational managers had told us how they were fed up writing reports and very often just sent in the same numbers as the previous month, or massaged the numbers to show favourable performance. The managers in the room listened intently and then one of them raised his hand and asked "On what premises have you based your decisions?" Many of them turned white when the presenter replied "On the data that you report each month."

Unfortunately, this is the reality of many organizations that collect and analyze vast amounts of data. They rarely ask the questions "What is this data telling us?" and "Is there anything we are going to do with this?" Much of the data that is collected is redundant, as either it is not reviewed or, if it is, it does not say anything new. As the head of curriculum and service improvement at a local authority once told us: "We don't measure what is valuable. We value what we measure."

Can the data be analyzed soon enough for action to be taken?

In performance measurement we often talk about lagging and leading indicators. Many companies rely on backward-looking data that has a time lag of at least a quarter, or at best a month. Lagging indicators are those that report on outcomes when it is often too late to do anything about the underlying causes. If, for example, every month you reported that you were definitely still alive, it would be too late to do anything about it when one month you reported that you had died! However, organizations constantly review such lagging indicators, believing that they are monitoring their performance. There would be no point reaching the end of the year to find out that you had not met the shareholders' expectations for financial returns. What organizations ought to be doing is using leading indicators to monitor the health of their business. For example, if each month you reported your blood pressure, cholesterol levels and liver function, the potential for an adverse outcome could potentially be avoided. Likewise, in an organizational setting you could report on customer complaints, backlog per department, payments collected, etc. However, consider what might happen if you have a complicated medical test and it takes three months for the results to be delivered, and in that time you die. This often happens in business situations where leading indicators are rightly used but the time it takes to collect the data, for example employee satisfaction survey data, is too long and your disgruntled employees have already taken strike action before the survey has been analyzed. Therefore, when making decisions on any data, the timeliness of your data should be a prime consideration.

Much information, however, can only be collected historically, and although there is nothing inherently wrong with this you should ask yourself whether the data that it produces can be collected, put through the right channels and analyzed quickly enough so it can still inform your decisions and actions.

Is the cost of collecting and analyzing data justified?

As we saw in the previous chapter, cost estimates of using performance measurement systems are rare and such systems are often implemented without any real cost/benefit analysis. Although we reported examples from private companies, it is not only commercial organizations that spend such high a percentage of their time and money measuring and reporting. The Spending Review presented by the UK government in 2004 included a total of 127 national Public Service Agreement targets. Ministries estimated that they spent up to £1.25m per target per year monitoring progress, and this excluded the costs of the front-line organizations providing the data.[9] This means that the cost of simply *monitoring* how ministries were doing against the national targets amounted to around £150 million; the cost of introducing the measurement systems, the software, the training of analysts and the gathering, analyzing and communication of the data was surely much higher!

Many organizations forget about the hidden costs of measuring performance. These costs are incurred in such areas as understanding the requirements of the performance measurement system; determining the extent to which current working practices require change; and ensuring that current systems and processes will produce the required data. Other, more variable costs of measurement, include such areas as managers having to learn the requirements of the system; the development of procedures for monitoring and measuring; the training of employees to understand the basic requirements of what needs to be measured and reported; and the reprogramming of computers or the purchase of new software to help with the measurement demands. For example, the small software company that wished to measure absenteeism, which we described above, ended up spending £40k in order to measure something that was of no benefit to the organization.

Will the measure encourage any undesirable behaviours?

One of the downsides of online shopping is the need to be at home when the delivery is made. Although the majority of companies will give you a tracking number so that you can see that the parcel has left the depot, there is nothing more frustrating than seeing that it has been returned to that same depot because nobody was at home. How come, after you stayed in all day, did nobody ever ring your doorbell? How or why does this happen? Recently, we discovered that one of the reasons may be because of the way parcel delivery firms measure and reward their drivers. Drivers are measured on the *attempt* at delivering a parcel, not on the actual delivery. Therefore, it is much more beneficial for the driver to *fail* to deliver your goods the first time around.

Another favourite example of measures that encourage unusual behaviour is the famous story of Vasili Alexeyev, the Russian super-heavyweight lifter. Vasili was offered a reward for every time he broke a world record. However, the measure never stipulated by how much the world record had to be broken, and therefore our sly Mr Alexeyev made sure he only *smashed* the record by as little as possible each time, in some cases by as little as a gram.

The greatest measurement madness is the unforeseen behaviours that are engendered in the human being measured. Much of this book is dedicated to unravelling the drivers of such behaviours and looking for an alternative, saner, way to use performance measurement. We will not dwell on this here. However, we do want to emphasize that when you look at your performance indicators, you must try to anticipate the behaviours that such indicators are likely to encourage.

Whether you are designing your indicators from scratch, or whether you are implementing performance indicators that have been thrust upon you, the Ten Tests of a Good Measure (summarized in Table 4.2) can help highlight the potential failure points of your indicator. We don't believe it is possible to design the perfect indicator, but if you understand the weaknesses in the measures that you utilize you can foresee some of the potential pitfalls.

Table 4.2 The Ten Tests of a Good Measure.

Test	Why is it important?
1. Is the indicator measuring what it is meant to measure?	To ensure that the indicator is valid, i.e., it measures exactly what it claims to be measuring.
2. Is the indicator only measuring what it is meant to measure?	To ensure that the indicator measures "the whole truth and nothing but the truth", i.e., it covers fully what it is meant to measure and doesn't listen to other "noise".
3. Is the indicator definitely the right indicator?	To check whether the indicator could introduce distortions and whether it could be replaced by a more appropriate one.
4. Is the indicator consistent regardless of who measures and when?	To ensure that the indicator is reliable and that results will not vary depending on who takes the measurement and when.
5. Can the data be readily communicated and easily understood?	If the indicator is to be used for making decisions, it must be calculated and reported in a timely manner and be easy to understand.
6. Is any ambiguity possible in the interpretation of the results?	Ambiguity makes decision-making slower and more difficult. The data provided by the indicator should be as clear as possible in order to minimize bias and reduce the risk of misinterpretation.
7. Can and will data be acted upon?	To ensure that the data provided by the indicator can and will in fact be used for making decisions and that time and effort is not wasted in measuring and reporting.
8. Can the data be analyzed soon enough for action to be taken?	To ensure that the procedures necessary to calculate the indicator can in fact be completed quickly enough to provide timely information for making decisions.
9. Is the cost of collecting and analyzing data justified?	To assess whether the time and resources that go into collecting, collating, analyzing and reporting the data are likely to be offset by the benefits that measurement brings.
10. Will the measure encourage any undesirable behaviours?	To prevent, or at least mitigate, the effects of potential dysfunctional behaviours.

LEARNING POINTS

As we have highlighted throughout this chapter, there are two aspects to learning about how to design and use performance indicators. The first learning points, as summarized in Table 4.1, are those you should consider when designing a performance indicator. The second set of learning points are those on how to test the validity and reliability of a new or existing indicator.

It's not just a KPI

As we mentioned earlier in this chapter, performance indicators are often seen as a panacea, a quick and fail-proof solution to performance-related issues. Indeed, if performance falls short of expectations, it seems that all we need to do is to tighten the measurement and bring the performance back under control. However, in our experience, this is no more than an automatic, knee-jerk reaction, which actually threatens to disrupt your organization's performance even further, whilst potentially costing you a substantial amount of money.

It is important to remember that performance indicators hold the power to disrupt and de-focus your organization just as they can provide a helping hand and enable organizational learning and, ultimately, performance improvement. Which way the cookie will crumble will depend on your willingness to think through the critical elements that determine the effectiveness of your performance indicators. Therefore remember these key points:

- Name the indicator appropriately;
- Be clear as to what purpose it serves;
- Think about what it relates to in terms of other indicators as well as the overall organizational goals;
- Make sure the way it is calculated is precise and clear;
- Think through how often you will take the measurement and review the results;
- Clarify the source of data for the indicator;
- Spell out explicitly who is responsible for measuring it, who takes action and what they are expected to do.

It should now be clear that using the so-called standard indicators from measurement catalogues and compendia is not likely to fully address your performance-related issues. Whether you go for an off-the-shelf indicator or develop your own, it is not "just a KPI".

Pass or fail

Sometimes, you don't have the luxury of introducing a new indicator into your organization. In that case, you need to channel your energy into understanding what you can expect from the existing metrics and how far they can take you. Working your way through the Ten Tests of a Measure will show you where your indicators can be a reliable guide in your performance management effort and where they are likely to encourage the darker side of performance measurement. The questions you should therefore ask of your indicator are:

- Is the indicator measuring what it's meant to measure?
- Is the indicator only measuring what it's meant to measure?
- Is the indicator definitely the right measure (for your purpose and context)?
- Is the indicator consistent regardless of who measures and when?
- Can the data be readily communicated and easily understood?
- Is any ambiguity possible in the interpretation of the results?
- Can, and will, the data be acted upon?
- Can the data be analyzed soon enough for action to be taken?
- Is the cost of collecting and analyzing data justified?
- Will the indicator encourage any undesirable behaviours?

Taking each of your indicators through these ten tests will give you an incredibly powerful understanding of the state of performance measurement in your organization, and the extent to which it is vulnerable to the bouts of measurement madness.

AND FINALLY...

Even after considering all of the points in this chapter, there is no accounting for the behaviour of managers when it comes to measurement. Recently, one of our colleagues found himself in a drawn-out argument with the operations manager of a small manufacturing company. The argument centred on whether the operations manager should be the one tasked with measuring the collection of late payments. Our colleague suggested that because collecting the money in arrears was an accounts-related indicator, it should be under the control of the finance director. However, after an hour long debate the operations manager refused to give in, and when finally our colleague asked "Why would you want to be responsible for measuring something that is not part of your remit and that you have no control over?", the exasperated operations manager spat out "Because I'm good at it!"

5

Comparing Performance

In 2007, an English secondary school was deservedly celebrating its success in the most recent GCSE (General Certificate of Secondary Education) examinations. The school's philosophy was to focus on the individual achievements of students; their success in progressing to university courses and fulfilling careers; and their holistic development. Therefore, the fact that pupils had achieved near perfect results, with only one pupil missing out in one particular subject, was indeed cause for self-congratulation. However, as the school was soon to discover, self-congratulation would be their only praise for this impressive achievement.

Shortly after the results, a league table[i] of schools was published by the Department for Children, Schools and Families (DCSF), which placed the school just within the top 25% of schools nationally, and which stated that only 75% of the pupils had in fact passed five or more GCSEs. Naturally, the school's head teacher and board of governors were aghast at this misrepresentation of their achievements and called for clarity on how this ranking had been calculated.

Although being congratulated, it was pointed out that whilst the benchmark of five subjects was consistently measured across all secondary schools, the pupils entered into the calculation had to be aged 15 on 1st September in the year prior to the examination. Therefore, the fact that this particular school allowed pupils to sit the examinations at the most appropriate time in their development, be this at a younger or older age, had counted against them in the ranking. As this particular school took in a number of pupils from overseas, the age of school development differed. For example, pupils from the southern hemisphere start their school year in January rather than the previous September.

More galling for the school was the letter, which explained that had the ranking only been in academic subjects, such as English, Mathematics, the sciences, etc., rather than vocational subjects, the school would have been placed in the top 10%. The school was also advised that as long as they sought to meet the needs of "each and every pupil", as had been publicized as good practice by a UK government

---

[i] Often described as a "ranking" in the USA.

report,[ii] their ranking would always misrepresent them. So much for providing a well-rounded, targeted and appropriate education. You may well ask, why be worried? Surely, for educators, the fact that students were achieving their potential should have been rewarding enough. However, league tables are powerful tools, as they inform parental and pupil choice, and sometimes determine funding and appointment or removal of school head teachers. This school would, therefore, suffer at the hands of the league table compilers, as the misrepresentation would in fact harm their ability to attract future students and endanger the school's very viability.

In our very first story, the supply chain director of Mike's company ended his presentation by showing a ranking of warehouse performance. What was so contentious about that choice? After all, the aim was to display information in a comparative way and to promote healthy competition between sites. Instead, it seemed to have had the opposite effect, with most people expressing doubts about the numbers and dissatisfaction with the process. As with the case of the English secondary school above, the league table was compiled in an unclear manner and people felt unfairly judged; just as no school is the same, because context matters, no warehouse is either, because strategies vary. For example, the "fast fashion" company Zara is known for underutilizing its warehouses and if we were to compare Zara with other companies using a benchmark of warehousing efficiency we would undoubtedly classify it as an inefficient company. However, to Zara this assertion would make little sense, because having warehouses half empty and keeping stock to a minimum is a clear consequence of their strategy for fast and flexible delivery.[1]

However, the use of league tables is not all doom and gloom. In many cases, as well as fulfilling the important role of providing crucial information on how an organization is performing vis-à-vis others, a comparative ranking process can also help an organization understand why its performance is better or worse than its competitors. Staying with education, a good example of this is the Programme for International Student Assessment (PISA) run by the OECD. Essentially, the

---

[ii] The Tomlinson Report, October 2004: https://www.education.gov.uk/publications/standard/publicationDetail/Page1/DfE-0976-2004

programme tests 15-year-old school pupils in 59 countries in mathematics, science and reading, with the overall aim to improve education policies and outcomes. The tests were first conducted in 2000 and have then been repeated every three years. The results are now widely publicized by the media and although these are often reported in simplistic, if not misleading, ways, PISA results have had a strong impact on education policies around the world. The results have triggered wider debates on the minimum levels of public funding, on the role of parents and family income on student attainment, and on the reasons for differences in scores between male and female students.

These stories illustrate a couple of basic factors to consider when using data to compare performance between different entities. Firstly, the data has to be collated and analyzed using the same rules; secondly, those being measured and those using the performance information need to understand on what basis comparisons and conclusions will be made; and, thirdly, those undertaking such an exercise should be using the results to look at ways to improve their performance, rather than worrying about their position. This is not only pertinent to institutional league tables, but also to commercial benchmarking.

In order to compare the current performance of your organization, or the product you sell and manufacture, or the ability and productivity of your people, you can use benchmarks. Benchmarking is a technique whereby you review the performance of others to judge your own performance, and then use that judgement to identify areas for improvement. However, there are a few key issues to consider when contemplating a benchmarking project.

The first issue with performance benchmarking is to consider who you are comparing yourself against. If you want to run in the main Olympics' 100 m final then it is not really useful to compare the time you take to run 100 m with David Weir's[iii] time over the same distance whilst he was racing in the Paralympic marathon. The second concern is that you need to know what your current level of performance actually

---

[iii] David Weir CBE was the British Paralympian who achieved four gold medals at the London 2012 Paralympics in the T54 class in the 800 m, 1500 m, 5000 m and marathon.

is. If you do seriously want to compete in the Olympic 100 m final, then you will need to know what the qualifying time is; you will then need to measure how fast you can currently run; and then work out a training program to improve your performance to where you need to be. Therefore, from an organizational perspective, if you want to compete in a particular market or geography, you need to know what the entry level performance criteria are. However, unlike the PISA tests, which are standardized and have clear and homogeneous measures and scoring systems, this may not be so easy in the commercial world. Also, the pitfall of establishing current performance is just that – it is only the current performance. As good financial analysts know well, one thing is sure about future performance: it will be different from past or current performance.

APPLES AND PEARS

The school league table story, recounted at the beginning of this chapter, illustrates a number of important points concerning the comparability of data, the first being that the outcome measures may well be different because the way the data are collected is not consistent. However, it is not sufficient that robust data are collected; the data should also be recorded in the same way.

Differences in data collection

On first coming to power, David Cameron, the British Prime Minister, made a bold pledge to reduce the number of heart-related deaths in the UK, as a benchmarking study had shown that the British were woefully behind other European countries in this area, especially France. On face value this appears to be a fair comparison. After all, countries in Europe have similar demographics, similar standards of living and, more often than not, similar standards of social healthcare. Why then, in comparison, were heart-related deaths so high in the UK? After all that wonderful French cheese, you would expect this statistic in France to be comparable to that in other European countries. Although many observers have labelled this phenomenon the French Paradox,[iv] on closer inspection it appears that it can also be attributed to the way the data are recorded. In the UK, when someone dies and the doctor is unsure of the underlying reasons, the physician will officially record heart failure as cause of death. However, in France, the doctors have a category for unknown cause of death, and only when the doctor is sure do they record the death as heart failure.[v] Therefore, making important decisions on the allocation of valuable public funds based on flawed comparative data is not wise. How often does this happen in organizations where different data are reported and decisions are taken on these incomparable datasets?

A trivial, but indicative example from the USA should prick the conscience of many organizations attempting to compare the performance of branches, departments, regions or even countries. A particular supermarket chain strived to benchmark one store against another and to check what lines sold well in particular areas. On reviewing the outcome of the data analysis, they were surprised to find that a particular inner city store sold more hard-boiled eggs than all of the other stores put together. Intrigued, the executives decided to carry our further investigation as to why people in this particular city ate so many hard-boiled eggs. On questioning a checkout worker, they asked how many hard-boiled eggs they had scanned that day. The checkout operative looked puzzled and reported that they hadn't sold any, and couldn't in fact remember ever having sold any hard-boiled eggs. Another worker, overhearing the conversation, then realized what had been happening, and gleefully reported what nobody else had seen. If the code on a piece of merchandise could not be recognized, but the checkout person knew the price then they scanned the code for hard-boiled eggs. For example, if a loaf of bread had lost its bar code, but they knew that it cost $1.50, and a hard-boiled egg retailed at 10 cents, then a loaf of bread was equivalent to 15 hard-boiled eggs. Of course, if the executives were only comparing the revenue of branches then there would be no problem.

[iv] The French paradox is the observation of low coronary heart disease (CHD) death rates despite high intake of dietary cholesterol and saturated fat.
[v] See the informative article on French Coronary Heart Disease at http://www.ncbi.nlm.nih.gov/pmc/articles/PMC1768013/

Likewise, if the people who scanned the products were aware of how the data were to be used, then they would have recorded it properly.

Precise definitions of the underlying data are crucial for any form of comparison. Another health-related example, concerning to survival rates of hip fracture operations, clearly illustrates this point. Research has shown that the chance of death after a hip fracture is high; therefore, there have been many studies as to how and why this occurs. Comparing hospitals for their mortality rates due to such an injury seems eminently sensible and should help to improve the performance of the poorer hospitals. However, an academic study has shown that survival rates of a hip fracture are dependent on the time between the accident and the treatment, not the treatment itself.[2] So, scoring hospitals on the outcome of their treatment would be incorrect and would probably lead to flawed decisions, as the most important measure in this case would be related to the timeliness, rather than to the effectiveness, of the operation.

Different datasets

It might be that data are similar, but if the datasets are not complete, this can once again lead to comparing apples with pears. A study, conducted in the UK by the Department for Transport, reported that: as a pedestrian you were 16 times more likely, and as a cyclist you were 12 times more likely, to sustain a serious injury than if you travelled to work by car.[3] This seems quite a surprising finding, but it is actually a great example of not comparing "like for like" datasets.[vi] First of all, people use these different modes of transport for different distances, but the report counted accidents per 1 billion kilometres travelled. It may, therefore, have been better to have counted the number of accidents per hour travelled, as obviously a car can cover far more kilometres in that time than a pedestrian. Secondly, another view could be that those walking to work tend to set out later in the day than those commuting by car, and different accidents are likely to happen at different times of the day. Interestingly, these numbers were reversed when the number of minor injuries for these three groups was compared. Why was this?

[vi] Dr Jennifer Mindel, a Health Research at University College London, discussed this eloquently on the BBC's *More or Less* radio programme on 3rd September 2010.

Well, not all pedestrian and cycle injuries will be reported. By law, in many countries, all car drivers must be insured and the insurers must be informed of any collision, however minor, as soon as one of the parties need to claim a repair or compensation for an injury. To add to the questionable viability of such data, in the UK there has been a substantial increase in false reporting of accidents in order to make fraudulent injury claims; to illustrate this statistic, although the number of road accidents dropped by 11% in 2012, the number of people claiming for an injury in a motor accident rose 18%, compared to 2011.[4] Therefore, whenever a car is involved in an accident the injury will be reported, whether truly sustained or not. On the other hand, if you are walking or cycling to work and fall over and sprain your wrist, such an accident may never be recorded, even if you attend the emergency room. Therefore, working on incomplete data does not give accurate reporting. In this case it would be best to compare similar modes of transport, similar roads, and similar times of day.

Many of these pitfalls also apply when considering the inputs, the processes and the outputs of a benchmarking exercise. Identifying those organizations to benchmark with is difficult, as you need to have significant information about those organizations to fully understand whether you are similar in nature, performance and outputs. Many organizations benchmark to learn about "best practice", but the very notion of "best practice" is questionable, as what is good for one may not be appropriate for another. Successful practices are often unique to an environment or situation, and it is very difficult to unpick the causal ambiguities and determine which practices in which contexts actually lead to success.

Different methodologies

Besides looking at the actual data compared in ranking and benchmarking exercises, it is important to understand the methodology used to calculate the final score or performance output. For example, there are numerous league tables, published in national papers, which attempt to compare the performance of universities within individual countries and across the world. However, the results of the published league tables can vary widely, even though they are based on the same data. The more reputable compilers do attempt to address this problem, carrying out robust comparisons by taking into consideration the different sizes of institutions, the demographics of their intakes, even the quality of the beer in the students' union bar, and adjusting the score so as to make it comparable.[5] More often than not, however, only the final figure is reported, keeping the process of compiling the league table far away from the reader's reach.

The GCSE example showed how organizations that make up a ranking table also need to understand the rules on how the table will be compiled. For example, if you are a university renowned for its high quality of teaching, you may not fare well in a league table that is focused on research income and outputs. Likewise, if you are a research intensive university, you may not fare well in a league table that measures teaching quality. This factor is not unique to education; it applies to all forms of comparisons. For example, companies competing in the same market strive to succeed, but they know that success does not require them to necessarily have the most efficient processes, the most recognizable and appreciated brands, the best social and environmental policies, and the best people and assets.

As well as understanding the criteria of comparison it is also essential to ensure that the statistical methods employed are valid. One such comparison, which makes the headlines on an annual basis in the UK, is the comparison made between private sector pay and pensions with those in the public sector. The publicized numbers are based on "average" earnings, which often show public sector workers in a much better position. But is this a meaningful comparison? Schools and hospitals typically employ highly qualified professionals, such as teachers, doctors and nurses, and have a high proportion of graduates whose income is relatively high compared with private sector industries such as retail, leisure and manufacturing. Even more bizarrely, following the recent bailout of several banks by the government, statistics on public sector workers have been distorted by the inclusion of highly paid bankers in these newly nationalized banks! However, the comparisons made and reported on do not take into account these differences and, because the focus is on averages, they do not truly represent the skew in highly educated professionals in the public sector with the more widely distributed mix in the private sector. As one commentator stated "it is like using the average pay of neurosurgeons and the average pay of bartenders to conclude that neurosurgeons are overpaid!"[6] But this is not the only element to consider; there are, of course, multiple factors at play. For example, public sector workers are on average older, and, because of their vocation, they remain in their profession for longer and therefore, due to length of service, command a higher salary than private sector managers at the same level. And what about bonuses? The bonuses of bankers and CEOs have had plenty of headlines, but the Office of National Statistics comparison figures discussed above do not even account for the £20 billion or so paid out in this way.

Interpretation and presentation

Finally, the usefulness of a public comparison, the utility of a commercial benchmarking exercise, or the value of ranking people or institutions in a league table, not only rely on the robustness of the data or the validity of the statistical analysis, but also depend upon the decision-making processes and evaluation criteria of those who will be interpreting the data. One evening, one of the authors, whilst having dinner with a cohort of postgraduate students, asked why they had chosen our particular course. As senior executives, they had, of course, chosen sensibly on course content, the reputation of the institution, and the knowledge that they would gain. However, the dining companions then started to discuss why they had chosen their undergraduate courses and, more interestingly, their alma maters. The most common reason, among the male students, was the ratio of male to female students. Obviously, an important piece of data that is often omitted from publicized league tables!

No amount of fancy number crunching footwork will eliminate the possibility that we are only being presented with a selection of data that delivers a particular message. Over the past decade, governments around the world, along with the scientific and popular press, have paid increasing attention to global warming. The argument that the average temperature of our planet's atmosphere and oceans is steadily rising has polarized expert opinion, even though the hard data is compelling. Sceptics, however, were fuelled by the actions of the Climatic Research Unit (CRU) of the University of East Anglia, which plays a leading role in compiling UN reports and tracks long-term changes in temperature, when the CRU refused to publish the underlying data. It was of no surprise when, in November 2009, we awoke to reports that hackers had broken into the CRU database to show that the data could be interpreted differently. The infiltrators were keen to expose the fact that eminent scientists had discussed, via email, the potential biases of the outcomes and messages.

However, it wasn't the climate scientists that were manipulating the data to support their messages; it was the hackers themselves who were selectively releasing the data owned by the CRU. By filtering the emails and selecting the ones that supported their viewpoint, they were able to build a credible case against the CRU, on which questions were asked in the highest political offices. This selective disclosure gave the impression of impropriety because the data had not been publicly available. The investigations into these claims examined email exchanges to determine whether there was evidence of suppression or manipulation of data by the researchers in the CRU. Eventually, the scientists were vindicated, but the hackers were not.

Although the manipulation of the data by the hackers was not to be applauded, their level of scepticism, over the presentation of the original data, was. A recent programme on BBC's Radio 4[7] promoted the idea of always being sceptical about the data presented. A renowned editor of a scientific journal warned that reviewers and readers of material should always be sceptical, because although scientists can run lots of experiments, they only need to publish the ones that support their hypotheses. This perceived bias, at the highest level of scientific endeavour, demonstrates that it would serve the general public well to increase their level of scepticism. And, if you are reading this from a managerial viewpoint, it begs the question: how sceptical are you when presented with good or bad news on how your organization compares with others?

Therefore, when reviewing comparative data we have to ask ourselves: is this the right data? Is there a difference between what is claimed and what was actually measured? What may have been left out? What has been added in to make the data look good? Just by changing a few assumptions in the models you can often get dramatically different outcomes. Therefore, not only should we be mindful of the way the data were collected in the first place, but we also need to maintain a healthy level of scepticism about the way results were compiled, presented and publicized.

TIMELINESS

The next question to be addressed is whether an apple today is the same as an apple eaten by the Romans or the Aztecs. The roundness, lack of insect infestation, smoothness and shininess of apple skins are the minimal requirements for today's consumers. Did our ancestors eat such perfect specimens? Probably not: even when comparing apples with apples, time is a fundamental factor to consider. From a managerial point of view, when comparing performance you need to ensure that the data can be analyzed soon enough to ensure that such a comparison makes sense.

We began this chapter by looking at the comparison of school examination data and stated that a school's position in a league table is important to attract future parents and pupils. However, should parents really be placing such store on this year's results? Any comparison of schools based on examination results is already out of date. Firstly, the results will not be known until at least two months after the examination was sat; then the compilation of the league table will take at least a couple more months, maybe even longer if the data are robustly verified. Therefore, if it took the student two years to study the course and it took the school a year to compile the results, then any choice being made today is already three years out of date; the equivalent of comparing a mouldy old apple with a fresh one. Interestingly, when looking at education league tables, the only people who seem to have a clear view are politicians: if you are in government and results are negative, you could always argue that the last government made a mess of education, and that your reforms are absolutely necessary. If you are in opposition, you could say that the results prove that the current government is making a mess of education, and that your return to office is vital.[8]

As markets evolve, using a static industry benchmark may not be useful as innovation (in technology, business models, etc.) may have made them outdated. For example, if we take the demise of the record industry we can see how benchmarking against competitors can have a negative effect. Since the rise of the CD in the late 1980s, the manufacturing of the casing, the disc and the artwork had become highly technologically driven. Music companies outsourced the manufacture of their CDs to third parties and their distribution channels to record shops were exemplary. The cost of a CD was often criticized in the media as it was deemed that it only cost 1 cent to create, yet $15 to buy. The production methods were benchmarked to destruction and each record company had honed their processes down to a fine art. What could possibly go wrong? Well, too intense a focus on benchmarking and continuous improvement had hindered the music industry's capacity to scan the external environment and detect groundbreaking technological changes. By the mid-2000s, the rise of digital downloads made the manufacture of CDs almost obsolete. Failing to update the benchmark and keep it relevant to the changing environment can blind an organization, or even an entire industry, and can have catastrophic consequences.

SPECIAL VARIATION

Despite warnings of an ever-increasingly warming planet, on 16th December 2009 heavy snow started to fall on London. Being a midweek afternoon, the disruption to homeward bound commuters was a major news item and bookmakers quickly slashed the odds of a white Christmas. Despite forecasts of a respite in the freezing conditions, the snow continued to fall, five Eurostar trains were frozen to a standstill in the Channel Tunnel, and eventually flights in and out of London's Heathrow international airport had to be abandoned. The notoriously critical UK press were soon baying for blood, demanding to know why Heathrow did not have sufficient snow clearing equipment and why had they not been better prepared. As most people accepted that this was a one-off anomaly, they decided to just enjoy the enforced holiday. However, almost a year to the day, in December 2010, the snow once again began to fall, and once again, despite the new investment in snow ploughs, Heathrow was forced to close.

The question then was, can heavy snowfall in December still be considered exceptional for London or is it becoming something we should expect? When comparing data, special variations are something to watch closely and to try to understand. The weather is a good example of this. Are we truly comparing like for like? Are we now to assume that all winters, or even more precisely, every second week in December will be snowy in London? Probably not, but it depends on the trends in the data. How long should we continue to collect trend data before we decide that a special variation is in fact the norm? How often in business do we explain away a bad quarter with our own special variations – it was unseasonably warm; employees went on strike; financial markets went crazy; the Olympics came to town – before we realize that the trends we are seeing are the new norm? Also, the time spent collecting data will impact our decision-making processes. One of the organizations we have worked with, a major oil company, told us that one of their key issues with measuring performance was that it took them 13 months to complete their annual budget. Obviously, tracing developing trends and taking timely decisions was out of the question!

CHOICE AND RELEVANCE

What made you choose where you live? Was it the political stability of the country? Was it the availability of work in the area? Was it the quality of the education and health system? Was it the average annual temperature? Well, here is one more piece of relevant data to add to your decision-making process. Scientists from the University of Southampton have recently created a league table of the countries that will be worst affected in the event of an asteroid strike. Economically developed countries are high up on the list due to the danger to their infrastructure, but so is China due to the sheer size of their population. In case this data is relevant to you in your decision-making process, the top ten countries most at risk are: China, Indonesia, India, Japan, the USA, the Philippines, Italy, the UK, Brazil and Nigeria. From a population perspective, the USA, China, Indonesia, India and Japan are most at risk, but Canada, the USA, China, Japan and Sweden would face the most devastation to their infrastructure. But how relevant is this data? Wouldn't you want to know how likely it is that the impact would be close to you?

When comparing data and expecting to make a choice, we must ensure that the data we are using are definitely robust and relevant to our choice. This point is well illustrated by the following example. The current trend in the UK is to give citizens more choice in their use of public services. However, this implies that citizens have enough data and are able to interpret the data correctly to make the most appropriate choice.

A friend of the authors recently gave birth, but, leading up to the delivery, she agonized over which hospital to choose. She studied the data, looked at the success of the natal unit, at the number of complaints, at the reputation of the doctors, at the statistics on cleanliness, at the choice of birthing options, and eventually made her choice on the one that didn't have road works on the main route to the hospital. An odd choice one might think, but this is the case with many decisions when there is too much data and it is not clear which is the most relevant. However, what would you have thought of her decision had she made it on the reputation of a particular consultant and then that consultant was on holiday the day she was admitted? Also, comparing the popularity of a hospital with another, when customers' choice is dependent on the condition of the local roads, is quite problematic. This is not unusual; often the data on which we are basing our choices has more to do with factors external to the organization and therefore it makes institutional comparisons difficult to interpret.

In business, the same issues arise. Market intelligence provides executives with data pertaining to market forces, customer population, customer segmentation and propensity to buy. A whole industry has been spawned on such data. However, as the example with the choice of hospital demonstrates, how relevant is all of this data when you are making strategic decisions? When interpreting and using performance data to inform decision-making, organizations should be selective in their choice of what is considered relevant, which can in part be determined by considering external factors that customers may find particularly useful.

USING DATA UNINTENDED FOR COMPARATIVE PURPOSES

The prestigious Lancaster University was recently placed at the top of a table for recorded "student cheating" among UK universities.[9] Lancaster reported 194 incidents, the University of East Anglia 187 and Bath University 182. But how meaningful were these results on a comparative basis? The data were collected under the Freedom of Information Act and all of the universities named agreed that the data were robust. However, the statement that Lancaster had the "worst record of cheating during the last academic year" was not entirely truthful or fair to the institution. The university may have been at the top of the table simply because it was more capable at detecting incidents of cheating. When Lancaster put an emphasis on the integrity of student output and created measures to monitor and improve their own performance in catching plagiarism and examination cheats, they probably did not expect those same measures to be used comparatively with other institutions.

So, how meaningful is the data? In this example, if the data were meant to measure the robustness and effectiveness of the detection systems, it should not have been used to report on the number of cheats. This was not what the data were intended for. The use of data for purposes other than what was intended can lead to a misinterpretation of the message. Therefore, when interpreting data we need to understand why the data were collected and how truthful the presentation of the findings is.

Another important point to make regarding league tables and benchmarking is that people whose performance is being compared should be aware of such comparison, and of the criteria used to make it. In a Nigerian company, which we have worked with in the past, the objectives for individuals are set by their immediate line managers. As with most conscientious employees, and especially those incentivized by performance-related bonuses, the individuals in this organization work extremely hard to achieve their targets. However, the organizational objectives and those at departmental, team and individual levels are often misaligned. This creates a very dysfunctional situation: the performance-related bonus is awarded to the department which contributes the most to the company's strategic goals, but this is almost unrelated to whether employees are achieving their own objectives. Even worse, the whole system is based on a benchmarking logic, but employees are unaware of the criteria used to perform the benchmarking exercise itself.

YES, BUT...

However hard we try, all comparisons will have limitations and inconsistencies, if only because humans will interpret the outcomes from their own psychological standpoint. The problem is that we all believe in our own publicity and our ability to delude ourselves is remarkable.

If a level of performance is ranked below that which was expected, the "yes, but..." reaction will surface a variety of reasons as to why the performance was deemed under par. There exists a social identity phenomenon whereby if your group, or team, compare favourably against other, similar groups, you will believe that it has been fairly compiled, you will be proud of the attainment of the team and you will "bask in the reflective glory". On the other hand, a slip of a number of places will be explained away by a criticism of the way in which the data was analyzed, you will not believe the standings, and you will "cut off from reflective failure".[10] As humans, we are very good at forcing meaning from data, particularly when that meaning confirms our prejudices and preconceptions. So, if we think we have had a good year and a comparison with peers reflects this, we will believe that the data are truthful.

Comparing performance in general, and benchmarking in particular, produces some very neat "yes, buts...". Also, companies will often benchmark individual units or parts of their business, rather than the organization as a whole. This makes sense, as it is meaningful to compare IT departments between different companies, but not whole organizations, if such IT departments sit in a construction company and a pharmaceutical one. Moreover, various industry accreditation bodies are increasingly awarding quality marks or certificates to say, for instance, that you are a people-focused business, based on just small parts of the organization. Benchmarking exercises only report on the individual items that are being measured, so you may have the best performing human resources department, but achieve the worst customer satisfaction scores; or you may have the highest performing sales team, but the poorest delivery mechanisms. This is analogous to the heptathlon or decathlon athletic events. A great heptathlete, such as Jessica Ennis-Hill, needs to obtain a high number of points in all seven disciplines. It would be no good if Jessica did really poorly putting the shot, but explained "yes, but...I ran a personal best in the hurdles".

MOVING UP THE RANKINGS

Whatever we feel about league tables, we need to consider whether a large jump up the rankings is a true reflection of increased performance?

Have you ever considered that the higher ranked you are, the less anything you do will affect that rank? This is why Oxford and Cambridge come out top nearly every year in UK university league tables. Why is it that these elite establishments are rarely overtaken? Similarly, why is it that the big four accountancy firms are never usurped by a lesser known outfit? A major reason is, of course, that success breeds success. Prospective students will potentially select those institutions that consistently top the academic league tables, which means that the leading universities will have more applicants and will be able to exercise greater selection. In a similar vein, if you are one of the elite soccer teams in Europe it probably means that you have spent vast sums of money buying the top players, bringing in the highest calibre coaches and providing state of the art training facilities. It will therefore take at least a decade of substantial investment before an outside club is taken as a serious contender for the title. Similarly, when comparing your organization's performance against others in your industry, you need to take into consideration your ability to attract top talent, the size and complexity of your operations and the length of time it takes for performance improvements to have an impact on the sector.

However, it is not only your ability to improve the underlying conditions that will advance your comparative standing; your position also depends on the number of league table entrants and the statistical significance of the ranking. To understand this phenomenon, consider the competitors in a marathon race. At the front of the race the runners may be nicely spaced apart, or maybe there will be small groups bunched together, just like the top universities in a league table. However, further back in the race there will be a continuous stream of runners. The ability to change position substantially in the middle of the field very much depends on the number of runners at that level of ability. For example, the New York marathon, one of the world's pre-eminent long distance running events, saw over 46,000 runners complete the course in 2012. If we were to compare the performance of the athlete who came 26,512th with the person who came 26,513th, could we categorically say that one was a significantly better runner than the other? Of course, we couldn't. Therefore, one of the key problems we have when interpreting a ranking is that we assume that differences in places are significant (being 54th is better than being 55th), but this is often not the case. In other words, just because your organization has moved up 20 places in a field of 300, does not necessarily mean that your performance has actually improved, even in relative terms.

Another good example is the ranking of Amazon reviewers. This may come as a surprise to you, but being an Amazon reviewer is something of a profession for some. There is an elite group of people who vie to be top of the reviewer rankings.[vii] Although many of us will leave a helpful comment on a product we have purchased, a "professional" reviewer will review at least 1000 products in a year. The reviewer rankings display a similar phenomenon to the marathon scenario, in that the people near the top have fewer ranking changes than those further down. If you are a top 10 reviewer you are likely to stay in the top 10; but not many of us would be able to spend the time and effort to break into this elite list; however, if you were to leave just 20 reviews you would quite likely jump up the table and make the top 10,000.

To sum up: can we really rely on what rankings tell us? Not really, as very often they only enable us to isolate performance at the extremes. Therefore, you can only use publicized comparisons as screening instruments to identify the best or worst product, institution, country to live in or hospital of choice. You cannot use rankings to make judgements on every individual item in the table. The problem is that we all overinterpret the results and jump to unfair conclusions about any major change in the rankings, whereas an apparent improvement in a low-ranked organization could just be a reflection of a regression to the mean – or, as others call this, a reversion to mediocrity. As an example, let's assume that your organization publishes a table of sales by individual salesmen. Now, all the salesmen have the same market to sell to, but some will be better at selling than others. The top salesmen will stand out, and the new, less experienced people will be at the bottom of the table. What about all the others, can you really rank them? If you look closely at the bulk of your sales team you will observe that the worst performing salesmen in the first quarter will tend to improve their figures in the second quarter and the better performers will tend to do worse in the second quarter. The phenomenon occurs because sales figures are determined, in part, by the underlying ability of the salesman and in part, by chance – in other words, being in the right place

---

vii See: http://www.amazon.co.uk/review/top-reviewers

at the right time. In the first quarter, some will be lucky, and sell more than expected; some will be unlucky and sell less than expected. Some of the luckier salesmen in the first quarter will be lucky again in the second quarter, but the majority of them will only sell their quota or even less than their quota. Therefore, a salesman who was lucky in the first quarter is more likely to have a worse record in the second quarter. Similarly, salesmen who sell less than the mean in the first quarter will tend to see their sales increase in the second quarter. This means that if we only look at quarterly sales performance, our conclusions about who is the best sales person is likely to be wrong.

Another important pitfall of comparing performance is that the mean could constantly increase and, despite improvements in performance, we would always find ourselves in the same position relative to the others. This effect is most obvious when the mean is used to calculate pay scales. This is one reason why the average pay of CEOs has rocketed in the past ten years. The average pay of a CEO of an S&P 500 company rose to $12.94 million in 2011 – a 13.9% increase over 2010. However, the pay of the top 1% in the pay scale grew by 11.6% whilst the income of the other 99% only grew by 0.2%.[viii] Put differently, the top 1% captured 93% of the growth in pay. This is because the principal mechanism used to determine and control high CEO pay is benchmarking against peer groups: as the pay of your peers increases, you are in a good position to ask for a pay rise. Consider this scenario: one senior engineer goes to his company bosses to complain that he is not being paid the same amount as his friend in the more generous company down the road. The organization, frightened of losing him, agrees to increase his pay to just above the amount his friend is earning. The day after, over a beer, the senior engineer tells his friend that he has just had a pay rise and that he is now being paid a more competitive salary, say, £2,000 a year more than him. This friend is rather perturbed and subsequently goes to his bosses to complain that he is no longer being paid a competitive salary. His bosses don't want to lose him, so they offer him a £4,000 pay rise, and so on.

Using external benchmarks can be useful, but they must be relevant to your organization's strategy. For example, in a recent review of long-term

---

[viii] For more statistics on CEO pay see: http://www.aflcio.org/Corporate-Watch/CEO-Pay-and-You/Trends-in-CEO-Pay

executive incentive schemes in Australia, the researchers found that, instead of designing pay packages that best reflected the needs of their companies, the boards tended to use standard performance measures for their executives. Advised by the same consultants and driven by the desire to benchmark, they were "herding" around ready-made solutions rather than thinking through what compensation packages they really needed.[11] This means that, in addition to the spiralling costs of executive compensation, described in the example above, companies are exposing themselves to the risk of being blinkered by a set of "standard indicators," which may or may not be critical for their business.

Increasing or decreasing your position in a league table, or improving your benchmark, may not be due to increased or decreased performance but due to differences or changes in the measurement system. A typical case is the one where organizations introduce more robust measures to capture their environmental impact: in several instances, the decision to report to the Toxic Release Inventory and ISO 14001 led to an apparent increase in emissions for many organizations, at least in the first few years of reporting. Similarly to the detection of university cheats described above, such increases were not due to worse performance, but to improved measurement practices. Therefore, in this instance, concluding that these organizations were "doing worse" would be incorrect, and certainly a drop in sustainability rankings would be unfair.

UNINTENDED CONSEQUENCES

When making comparisons you also need to ensure that, by creating a set of criteria, you are not changing the behaviour of the participants. In this chapter we have identified several forms of league tables: in sport, in the public sector, in education and in the private sector. Each of these tables is based on set criteria and in some circumstances behaviours have changed for the good to ensure a better ranking; for example, universities are more focused on the student experience, hospitals are more concerned with patient outcomes and businesses are more focused on customer satisfaction. But what happens when the league table changes the behaviour to something that was neither hoped for nor expected?

Perverse behaviours, such as hospitals moving patients from one area of the hospital to another to manipulate waiting times and climb the rankings, occur when league table participants only focus on the criteria of the table, rather than on what they are trying to achieve. The opening story to this chapter about the school that focused on the achievements and all-round abilities of their students is a classic example of this problem. League tables incentivize schools to behave in ways that benefit the institution rather than the pupils. As we have discussed, it is difficult to change the very top or very bottom participants in a ranking, and therefore schools have been known only to focus on the borderline pupils, helping them jump over the threshold grade, whilst neglecting the brighter or less able students.[ix]

As we have seen in this chapter, in order to improve your position in a ranking, you can not only improve results by enhancing people's abilities, for example training them harder for a marathon, but you can also change the measurement system or criteria. For example, very often governments celebrate the news that school children are improving in their academic ability proven by their examination results. However, one criticism is that this is not because children are more intelligent, but rather because examinations are getting easier. Gaming the league table system is one way of improving school results, and one of the easiest ways for a school to show an improvement in performance is to move their pupils to an easier examination board. One problem with this system is that, in the UK, for example, the examination boards actually have to compete against each other. They are commercial enterprises and therefore want to attract schools to use their examinations, and one way to do this is to make the examinations easier than the competitor boards. This can be taken to extremes, as demonstrated by the furore that erupted in 2012 when examination boards were exposed for attracting schools by giving away the content of the upcoming examination papers.[12]

[ix] The UK government has recently announced that from 2016 schools will be measured on overall results in eight subjects and that there will be four key league table measures, showing pupils' progress as well as final grades. The move has been hailed as a way to discourage the "damaging obsession" with the C grade boundary (see for instance Kirkup, J. (2013) Gove considers shake-up of exam results to stop the manipulation of league tables, *Daily Telegraph*, 1; National, 4).

If the aim of the examination boards is to help the students gain the highest grades possible, then it would be questionable as to whether the content of the examinations is focused on the most appropriate education for young people. The current system has been criticized for testing knowledge rather than understanding, and for encouraging schools to perversely enrol pupils in easy subjects and only teaching them the facts that will enable them to answer the examination questions. This leads to the problem that employers have no idea of a school leaver's cognitive ability, only their ability to learn and regurgitate facts.

Outcome-driven comparisons, such as examination results, will often lead to unintended behavioural consequences. Gaming of outcomes is always a possibility if input measures and ongoing process measures are ignored. For example, a hospital that is measured and compared purely on the outcomes of patients' survival rates may not even admit patients if they are high risk. The most experienced heart surgeons in the country are much more likely to be given the most difficult cases, but that may mean that their patients' survival rates are much lower. Is it likely then that a highly rated heart surgeon would turn down these complicated cases? Reflecting on school success, if difficult or less able pupils are excluded from school, they won't count in the outcome measures of examination success. Such a situation is actually real, and it has led to reports of a small number of schools using selection and exclusion as a means of improving their position in a league table. A target-driven, league table-obsessed culture means that institutions care more about results than how those results are achieved.

Finally, although in many cases such measurement madness is amusing rather than critical, when it relates to human lives, it warrants more serious concern. Consider, for example, the comparative reporting of mortality rates of stroke victims in US hospitals. If a patient is admitted with a stroke, or has a stroke whilst in hospital, the hospital is measured on how many of those patients die in the hospital because of their condition. Unfortunately, because the measure is not extended to patients who die once they are sent home, it has been reported that in Californian hospitals the tendency is to discharge patients early so that any subsequent deaths are not counted in the comparative data.[13]

LEARNING POINTS

The madness that may ensue when trying to compare your organization against others in a league table or against similar organizations in a benchmarking exercise has been clearly illustrated with some of our stories in this chapter. Comparing performance has many pitfalls, ranging from the type of data to collect; the collection mechanisms employed; the consistency of the data with whenever or whoever measures; and the reporting of the outcomes without ambiguity. So how can you avoid these pitfalls? Table 5.1 summarizes the steps you can take to get the best information from your comparative data.

Table 5.1   A summary of the steps you can take to get the best information from your comparative data.

Pitfalls	Remedies
1. Collecting the wrong data	Work out what you want to compare, which will inform your strategy.
	Do not make comparisons just because the data are readily available.
	Have a plan – what data do you need to collect, how will you collect it, and what will you compare with whom?
2. Only taking superficial meaning from the data	Collect qualitative data for deeper insight.
	If you only collect quantitative data then ensure you build a narrative around it.
3. Data is inconsistent	Always measure and record in exactly the same way as your comparators.
	Do not just compare outputs; try to understand the processes that created those outputs.
4. Ambiguity is never considered	Do not make assumptions around the mean.
	Do not take data at face value; consider the causal factors that led to the number.

Which data to collect?

The first lesson is to refrain from collecting data just because they are easy to collect or readily available. In this day and age the most common pitfall is to collect data because the technology will allow it. In order to avoid this trap you should firstly identify why you want to compare your institution or your performance against others'. Secondly, create a plan of what you are going to compare, how and with whom; and thirdly, remember that any benchmarking exercise should be aligned to your strategic objectives. Wherever possible, a benchmarking exercise should compare whole organizations or systems, as this can help mitigate potential gaming and perverse behaviours. However, when it is only possible to compare specific units, functions or processes, you should be very clear in the definition of what you are comparing, understand all the inputs and processes involved and specify the boundaries of the comparison. Then, and only then, should you establish the data you will collect. Finally, choose appropriate benchmarking partners who have comparable data to yours and remember to compare apples with apples.

Collection mechanisms

The second lesson is to work out how you are going to collect the data. Whichever data collection mechanisms you choose, you need to ensure that you rigorously plan and pilot the instruments you will use.

Straightforward quantitative data that can be gathered via a simple instrument, such as a survey, are easier to collect than qualitative data and are, these days, relatively cheap. Online survey tools are simple to use and make the dissemination of the survey very cost effective. However, be aware that what looks simple, straightforward and cost effective can lead to more extensive and expensive analysis. More importantly, from a measurement madness perspective, numbers can be far more easily manipulated.

If you wish to collect rich data that will hopefully inform your decisions, then the identification and collection of qualitative data is far more beneficial than a survey. As we have seen in this chapter, interpreting and then explaining quantitative data often has to be accompanied by a narrative to ensure that the reader understands all the nuances involved. Unfortunately, the gains in richness from qualitative data collection mechanisms often come at a much higher cost and longer timescales.

Consistency

As we have seen throughout this chapter, comparisons only make sense if data are collected and analyzed consistently. Firstly, ensure that, if you are comparing two organizations, measurement is undertaken in exactly the same way, as illustrated by the story about heart-related deaths in France and the UK.

If you are benchmarking against another organization then the work needed to achieve consistency will be very detailed. Therefore, you may need to analyze whether the benefits you are likely to obtain will be worth the cost of the work. If you believe you can do a quick and dirty comparison, then do not overanalyze the findings and try not to make important organizational decisions on that data.

It is often impossible, in a benchmarking or comparison exercise, to be able to identify or gather information on the relationships that exist within an organization, let alone work out how they affect the outcome indicators. Also, not everything that happens in your organization is under your control; how people work together and how processes evolve are often difficult to manage. Therefore, just comparing output data will not tell you a great deal about how those results were reached. Although understanding the processes that created the outputs is crucial, the cost of comparison and ensuring data consistency can often outweigh the benefits.

Handling ambiguity

The reporting of findings in league tables and the recommendations for continuous improvement that often follow are only as good as the data used and the models employed. Likewise, we have shown that, even with all other things being equal, you can still not make fine comparisons for the majority of institutions or organizations in the middle of a league table. So, although you may be able to continually refine the criteria, it is safer not to make assumptions about organizations around the mean. Therefore, you should exercise great care and sensitivity when concluding that there are apparent differences in performance between two different entities.

Using data to make informed decisions about your organization is definitely sensible; however, be very careful about how much weight you give to the data in making that decision. Suppose that, after conducting a benchmarking exercise, you believe your R&D department is underperforming; in addition, further data highlights the fact that your investment in R&D is in the lower quartile compared with your competitors. Rather than jump to an immediate conclusion to throw more money at the problem, you need to consider whether your competitors have the same R&D strategy as you, and if so, what other causal factors may be driving their R&D output. In most cases, being able to unwind the ambiguity of cause and effect is a better starting position.

AND FINALLY...

Although we have focused on the pitfalls, please do not be dissuaded that comparative information can be of immense value. The key lesson from this chapter is that, when using data to guide improvements in performance, extreme care is needed, and before carrying out any comparisons, you must ensure that all data is starting from the same premise. However, you may not want to go as far as this to establish the reliability of your data – a joke, which was recently voted one of the funniest in the world:

> Two hunters are out in the woods when one of them collapses. He doesn't seem to be breathing and his eyes are glazed. The other man pulls out his cell phone and calls emergency services. He gasps to the operator, "My friend is dead! What can I do?" The operator in a calm, soothing voice replies, "Take it easy. I can help. Firstly, let's make sure he's dead."
>
> There is a silence and then a shot is heard. Back on the phone, the hunter asks, "OK, now what?"

PART
III

Performance Management

6

Target Turmoil

Saturday evenings in the accident and emergency (A&E) department[i] in UK hospitals are notoriously busy. The waiting rooms are filled with amateur sports men and women with sprained or broken limbs; with the walking wounded who have injured themselves attempting home improvements; with revellers too drunk to be left safely on their own; and with small children having swallowed something they shouldn't have. After long tedious hours of waiting, tiredness and weariness soon set in. This used to be so bad that it was a commonly held belief that a broken limb would heal whilst waiting to be fixed, or that the drunk would have had long enough to sober up.

Shortly after winning the 1997 election, the New Labour government set out to reform the National Health Service (NHS) in England.[ii] To ensure consistent standards throughout the country, the government introduced national targets that would become enforceable across the whole sector. The most notorious target of all was that imposed on A&E departments to improve waiting times. The target was set at four hours and covered the period of time from a patient's arrival in A&E to the completion of treatment or admission into an inpatient ward. This target was designed to address citizens' growing dissatisfaction with the length of the waiting time in NHS hospitals. At the turn of the millennium, an interim target of 90% compliance with the A&E target was set, with the intention of reaching 100% by March 2003. However, there was a real lack of progress on achieving the target, and consequently by 2005 the target was revised to 98%.

Even if 98% is not 100%, achieving such a level sounds like a huge improvement. However, to ensure that at least 98% of all patients attending A&E were seen within four hours, some A&E departments introduced new arrangements. Notably, many would move a number of waiting patients into what was known as a clinical decision unit (CDU). Essentially, these were temporary assessment areas where patients could be pseudo-managed whilst ascertaining their underlying medical needs. Upon admission to the CDU such patients no longer counted as

---

[i] The same as the emergency room (ER) in the USA.
[ii] Within the United Kingdom, different performance measurement frameworks were implemented, this is why we are referring to England, rather than to the whole of the UK.

waiting, according to the national rules pertaining to the performance target. In reality, there was no major tangible difference between patient management and treatment in the CDUs and in the more traditional A&E setting. In some hospitals, the only such difference was a line on the floor of A&E demarcating the two different treatment areas. However, patients waiting for treatment in non-CDU areas were classified, by the national rules, as still waiting and therefore did count towards achieving the target.

Strangely, hospitals could also charge a differential rate (higher-cost tariff) for treatment of CDU patients than they would have received for non-CDU attendances. Therefore, for hospitals, this new arrangement had the double benefit of securing additional revenue while relieving the demands on A&E and their 98% performance target. Furthermore, the treatment outcome, care quality and speed of delivery was, in many cases, not actually superior to that which would have been experienced in the non-CDU setting; the X-ray of a broken leg and a colourful plaster cast were no different on either side of the divide. The creation of the CDU was therefore a technical workaround, managing the flow of patients in a way that ensured achievement of the target while maximizing income, but not necessarily providing better patient care.

In the public sector, targets have been identified as the primary cause of the growing disconnect between the way organizations operate and the best interests of the citizens and consumers of the service.[1] However, dissatisfaction with performance targets is equally common in private companies. In our introductory chapter, the chief operating officer in Mike's company denounced the use of performance targets and their related rewards as bribery, which had corrupted the ethics of his people. Similarly, the CEO of their IT subsidiary spoke about the dysfunctional consequences – in the form of gaming and cheating – of target setting.

Madness arising from target setting was also evident in a small pharmaceuticals company we worked with in Russia. There, the purchasing manager was perplexed at receiving large shipments of unordered medical products from India. A closer investigation revealed that these shipments were made by Indian suppliers of pharmaceutical products, who were under pressure to meet their sales targets. In order to meet or even exceed their targets, they would simply send boxes of medicine to Moscow, relying on the fact that shipping, acceptance and the ensuing investigation and return would take longer than their sales target horizons. The most ingenious of them would ship the products by sea!

Another, more light-hearted example of such dysfunctional consequences comes from a curry restaurant in Scotland. Going out for a curry is a pastime enjoyed by the majority of British people. Most casual Indian restaurant diners will choose a dish suitable to their palate, and will shy away from the hottest dishes on the menu. However, in October 2011, the emergency services were called to an Indian restaurant in Edinburgh after competitors engaged in the "world's hottest chilli" curry eating competition started feeling very, very sick. One of the participants was so ill that she had to be taken by ambulance to the Edinburgh Royal Infirmary, twice! The curry house owner said that he might have overestimated the participants' capacity and set the target too high, but felt the competition had gone well as the restaurant donated 25% of each serving's price to charity. However, he did admit that he might have to "tone down" the contest in future.[2]

While such behaviours are clearly extreme, in a recent survey of sales forces in private firms, the majority of respondents stated that the perceived impact of performance targets on behaviour was predominantly negative, and 53% of respondents expressed dissatisfaction with performance targets overall[3] – no wonder when you consider the Russian/Indian example and the consequences of the curry eating contest!

WHAT ARE PERFORMANCE TARGETS?

In general, a target refers to a specific level of proficiency, typically within a defined time limit, for example the number of cars sold per month or the number of phone calls answered per hour. Although target[iii] setting is an established practice, we owe a proper formalization of targets' roles and uses to Edwin Locke and Gary Latham's goal-setting theory. These authors describe a target as not only something we try to accomplish, but also something that regulates our behaviour and can give a sense of purpose to our actions.[4] Eating as much hot curry as

---

[iii] Since the terms "targets" and "goals" are often used interchangeably, in this chapter we will use the term "target", unless quoting material where "goal" is preferred.

possible demonstrates that a target can provide purpose to an otherwise meaningless and dangerous task, because it gives us something that we can try to achieve.[4] Although a target can lead to behaviour, which is pretty rational and harmless, burning a hole in your stomach lining is a dysfunctional consequence of target setting we would like to avoid. On the other hand, it could be much worse, as in the cases of corporate disasters in which extreme behaviours have decimated established international companies, ruining many innocent lives and leading to long-term prison sentences.

The story of Enron's demise has been catalogued in many books and papers, but it is a clear example of what can go wrong when targets drive dysfunctional behaviours. Enron was founded in 1985 and grew to be the seventh largest company in America. In the late 1990s, Enron diversified its business from the core distribution of power to more intangible business arenas such as the selling of Internet bandwidth and weather derivatives. During this time, the business diversified and so did its accounting methods. Enron was permitted by the federal regulators to use an accounting method called "mark-to-market", which allowed it to count estimated earnings against targets as current income. This peculiar use of targets allowed Enron to inflate its revenue projections and keep its share price high. In addition, in order to meet Wall Street expectations, Enron was busily buying up new ventures and turning them into profit centres while at the same time forming off-balance-sheet entities so that existing debt could be moved off the core balance sheet. In order to meet growth targets implicitly set by investment analysts and to keep their long-term share values high, the Enron executives used the company's shares to hedge its investments in their other entities. Inevitably, when one of the cards fell, the whole house came tumbling down.

Examples of perverse behaviours and unintended consequences of setting targets abound in both public and private sector organizations, cut across sectors, and have no geographical borders. If you look at the raft[iv] of newspaper articles, reports and academic papers that have

---

[iv] Funnily enough, the *Cambridge Dictionary* uses the following sentence to exemplify the meaning of "raft": "We have designed a whole raft of measures to improve the transport system", just in case somebody thought that to improve the transport system only a few measures were enough!

focused on target setting you will soon realize that issues like the ones experienced by the organizations mentioned above are quite frequent. These opening stories demonstrate the creativity of individuals and organizations in playing the target game. However, if performance targets drive such dysfunctional behaviour, why do organizations keep introducing them? And, if targets are here to stay, do we simply accept that sooner or later they will cause trouble, or can they actually be beneficial? In this chapter, we examine whether performance targets are good, bad or simply a lesser evil, and then discuss the key issues to bear in mind when introducing them. We conclude by providing recommendations on how to set and use targets.

WHEN TARGETS GO BAD

From healthcare to banking, from salesmen to school teachers, the use of targets is often associated with bizarre incidents. In some cases, they may lead to relatively minor consequences, as with the curry contest. In others, targets can be responsible for catastrophic failures, as the Enron case demonstrates.

If we look at the range of experiences and research on performance targets, we can see how these tools are likely to cause the most damage when they encourage individuals to focus on something that is disconnected from the issue at hand. The controversial case of the Ford Pinto, in the 1970s, is a good illustration of this point. According to the then Ford CEO, Lee Iacocca, "the Pinto was not to weigh an ounce over 2,000 pounds and not cost a cent over $2,000". The aim of producing a lighter and cheaper car is certainly commendable. The use of 2,000 pounds and $2,000 as targets (in this case intended as maximum admissible levels) eventually resulted in a series of positive achievements in terms of speed to market, fuel efficiency and cost savings. However, such targets also spurred perverse and sometimes unethical behaviours, which resulted in much reduced safety, and loss of human life and of company reputation.[5] Indeed, after being on the market for a few years, the Ford Pinto came under attack due to the number of deaths, which were allegedly linked to flaws in its design. An article in the *Mother*

Jones magazine argued that Ford was aware of all of the issues, but had refused to pay for a redesign, because the company had calculated that it would be cheaper to pay for the possible lawsuits and compensate for the resulting deaths than to carry out the required work. According to a cost/benefit analysis, Ford had estimated the cost of reinforcing the rear end of the car to be approximately $121 million, which was substantially higher than the potential $50 million payout to victims. Eventually, the Ford Pinto was associated with 53 deaths, many more serious injuries and very costly lawsuits.

The loss of human life can also happen in those institutions that actually have a mandate to do just the opposite. Over the past decade, many hospitals in the UK have been working towards the goal of obtaining "Foundation Trust" status; to be awarded such an accolade, a hospital has to demonstrate that it is in complete control of its finances and able to achieve government targets. Hospitals want the autonomy of becoming a trust as it gives them more freedom to act and the ability to borrow funds. One such hospital, in Mid Staffordshire, is a chilling example of how targets can make organizations "stupid".[6]

Problems began to emerge at the Mid Staffordshire hospital in 2007 when a report identified that it had unusually high mortality rates for emergency care. The healthcare watchdog, the Healthcare Commission, found that mortality rates were between 27 and 45% higher than average, equating to between 400 and 1,200 deaths more than expected. As it was later found, in the accident and emergency department, the initial assessment of the seriousness of the patient's condition was left to the reception staff, and seriously injured people were often left waiting covered in blood, some in soiled clothing, with no food or drink and, in some cases, no pain relief. One apocryphal story reports that some patients were so thirsty that they resorted to drinking water from flower vases. Relatives reported that overworked and inexperienced nurses shouted at patients, and doctors were diverted from seriously ill patients to deal with the bulk of more minor injuries in order to ensure that the national four-hour waiting time target would not be breached. Not surprisingly, Mid Staffordshire was one of the hospitals that employed the clinical decision unit technique we discussed earlier in order to stop the clock on the more seriously ill patients.

The hospital was under so much pressure to save tens of millions of pounds from its budget, to hit government targets, and to ensure it achieved Foundation Trust status, that it had lost sight of its mission, and the care of its patients had become secondary. By pursuing these targets, not only did healthcare workers forget about patient care, they were actually responsible for the deaths of hundreds of treatable patients. In 2014, following a series of investigations and reports, Mid Staffordshire Trust was eventually dissolved.[7]

Although missing targets in a business setting may not always kill the key stakeholders, missing financial targets can impact the share price for years to come; as we saw with Enron, the manipulative massaging of the figures can actually sound the death knell for the organization. The case of Informix is also indicative. In the 1990s, Informix was the third largest database maker in the world. However, losing market share to its major competitors, Oracle and IBM, was negatively impacting the achievement of its own financial targets, as well as the positions and stock options of its senior executives. Desperate times led to desperate measures. In order to boost their numbers, the executives booked revenues before sales were completed, and structured loose barter agreements with customers. Through such deals, Informix inflated its net income, thus increasing its share price.[8] However, these practices were eventually discovered, Informix's share price fell sharply and the Securities and Exchange Commission accused managers and sales personnel of focusing on targets rather than on securing new business.[9] Eventually, Informix had to pay $142 million to settle lawsuits resulting from SEC charges for fraudulently increasing earnings by $295 million in the 1994–1997 period. The company was then restructured and its majority sold to IBM.

ARE TARGETS SO BAD?

Do targets always engender such bad behaviour? Following a series of empirical studies, Locke, Latham and colleagues concluded that goal setting is *beneficial*, and that benefits can be proven time and time again. Indeed, 90% of their studies showed positive or partially positive effects of target setting both in experimental and in real-life settings.[4] Other authors reached similar conclusions. Having seen the catastrophic consequences of target setting in several organizations, such conclusions seem quite odd: how could this possibly be?

This chapter opened with the case of waiting times targets in accident and emergency departments in the English National Health Service. The performance measurement regime adopted by the New Labour government led to the publication of performance data at hospital level and to sanctions for poor performing managers, so much so that it was dubbed the "targets and terror regime" by its critics. However, despite its limited popularity, certainly among healthcare managers, and the numerous attacks it was subject to, this target-driven approach did lead to quite positive results overall. Indeed, recent research conducted in the UK and in the USA shows that hospitals striving to achieve their targets improved their performance both in absolute and in relative terms. In particular, Steve Kelman and John Friedman of Harvard University found dramatic wait-time performance improvements between 2003 and 2006 and no evidence of any of the dysfunctional effects hypothesized in connection with this target.[10] Carol Propper of the University of Bristol and her colleagues, in their comparative study of English and Scottish hospitals, found the performance measurement regime introduced in England lowered the proportion of people waiting for elective treatment relative to Scotland.[11] Several other reviews of the use of target setting in both private and public sector organizations show that, by and large, targets will help organizations improve their performance.[3] Therefore, contrary to the doom and gloom stories reported thus far in this chapter, targets have repeatedly been found to help provide focus, communicate priorities and motivate people.

THE MAIN PITFALLS

If targets have been proven to be beneficial to many, then why did they cause such madness in Enron, Informix and some English hospitals?

Although targets are quantitative representations of desired levels of performance, the main problems are not to do with strictly technical aspects, but with the behaviours and attitudes of the people affected by them. Moreover, even though we can observe the phenomena at the organizational or even at the industry level, it is the individual and team levels that we need to investigate if we want to understand the causes of the failures and if we want to find possible remedies.

Let's look at the main pitfalls of performance targets and the best ways to avoid them. The first area of concern is that targets can cause damage when they are introduced for control purposes. Although it is perfectly legitimate to monitor how an organization is doing, especially in important functions or areas, the dream of knowing and controlling everything that moves can soon transform itself into a nightmare of window-dressing, unsustainable improvements and dysfunctional behaviours. This is exactly what governments in various countries have experienced over the past two decades when trying to control everything from the centre.

Tired of constantly muddling through and bureaucratic inefficiency, over the past 15 or so years, the governments of many European and North American countries have attempted to introduce performance measurement systems at different hierarchical levels to try to ensure consistency between national policies and local service delivery. For example, during his first term, President Obama expressed his commitment to performance management when he called for the creation of

> "a focused team within the White House that will work with agency leaders and the White House Office of Management and Budget to improve results and outcomes for federal government programs while eliminating waste and inefficiency. This unit…will be…headed by a new Chief Performance Officer (CPO) who will report directly to the President. The CPO will work with federal agencies to set tough performance targets and hold managers responsible for progress. The President will meet regularly with cabinet officers to review the progress their agencies are making toward meeting performance improvement targets."[12]

Therefore, targets, with their rational appeal and numerical simplicity, play an important part in these governmental systems; however, no one administration ever bet more on the success of target setting than the UK's New Labour administrations of 1997–2009.

The New Labour government introduced the idea of a national target, which could be cascaded down to local delivery agencies, so that priorities would finally be clear and improvements measurable. This applied not only to healthcare, as seen in the example of the four-hour waiting target in A&E, but to all other government agencies. The approach of using targets was contested by many commentators, but often for the wrong reasons. It is generally accepted that, in its first term, the Blair administration did introduce too many targets at all levels, clogging up the system with sometimes valueless reporting. However, it is not because the targets were bad *per se* that the improvements were hard to achieve; it was mainly because of the top-down perspective adopted.[13]

Metaphorically speaking, performance targets, and measurement more generally, were regarded as the strings that the puppeteer could pull to stage a good performance. Although one can understand and sympathize with this view, in practice it is often clear that straight lines of communication and chains of command are not so easy to establish.[v] Rather, those strings start to seem more like a bundle of overcooked spaghetti: difficult to extricate, easy to break and hard to swallow. A poignant illustration comes from police forces. In Chapter 3, we touched on the problems generated in recording crime figures and referred to the recent inquiry, from the UK Parliament's Public Administration Committee, which led to the identification of "a system of incentives in the police that has become inherently corrupting".[14] Political pressure to reduce crime statistics, often exerted through performance targets, has resulted in crimes being downgraded to less serious offences or even in their "disappearance", as in the case of burglaries and even of sexual assaults; policemen admitted that they would try to persuade a victim that she had not been raped.[15]

A second area of concern for bad behaviour is linked to the challenging nature of targets. Proponents of performance targets have always stressed the importance of introducing targets that challenge current

---

[v] Please note that we are not denying the importance of alignment in functions and behaviours; we are simply arguing that targets are not magic wands that can be waved to quickly resolve very complex matters.

practices and performance. But how challenging should they be exactly? Well, in some cases apparently too much, as they can end up promoting a culture of unhealthy competition within organizations, excessive risk-taking and unethical behaviour. One of the first studies on target setting, conducted in 1951, looked at the introduction of an individual incentive plan, which linked pay increases to sales volume, in an American department store. To their surprise, the authors found that such scheme had resulted in the desired increase in sales volumes, which was good, but also in a deterioration of stock inventory and merchandise displays. Because performance was relative (in this case customer advisors were ranked) it was not only beneficial to individuals to increase their own sales volumes, but also to stop colleagues from selling more than them. Employees had become so uncooperative that they were stealing sales from one another and hiding highly desirable items so that they could sell them during their own shifts.[16]

More recently, the UK Financial Conduct Authority (FCA) found that pressure to achieve financial targets at Lloyds, Bank of Scotland and Halifax had created a "culture of misselling" products to customers. Looking at Lloyds' sale of investment products in the years 2010 to 2012, the FCA found that sales staff were offered "champagne" or "grand in your hand" bonuses for hitting targets.[17] At the same time, missing targets would result in dire consequences; so much so that the FCA found "evidence that one Lloyds staff member sold protection products to himself, his wife and a colleague to prevent himself from being demoted".[18] In 2013, taxpayer-backed Lloyds had to set aside more that £8bn to compensate victims of Payment Protection Insurance misselling; by far the largest provision ever made by any British bank.

Targets that are too challenging can also lead to data manipulation, which is a distortion of the facts related to the attainment of the desired levels of performance. The case of Lucent, an equipment manufacturer in the telecommunications business, is a good example of how to make the numbers when people are under extreme pressure. Before the scandal made newspaper headlines, Richard McGinn, former CEO of Lucent, proudly stated that imposing "audacious" targets on his managers produced "dream" results.[19] Under McGinn, Lucent, as many other publicly quoted companies, was driven by Wall Street expectations, and because these expectations were not managed properly, they were actually beyond the capacity of what the company could achieve.

Attempts to meet these unobtainable targets meant that the company started making special, expensive deals with customers at the very end of each quarter, to increase revenues counted in that period in order to make it look better than it would have otherwise.

However, this also meant that success in one quarter put considerable pressure on the following one. It was a classic case of robbing Peter to pay Paul. This meant that the company then needed "pull-ups" that soon escalated to "miracles". Because McGinn had been overpromising, as had happened at Informix and Enron, he had fraudulently misled investors.[20] According to Henry Schacht, who took over as interim CEO after McGinn was sacked, what happened to the company "is that our execution and processes [had] broken down under the white-hot heat of driving for quarterly revenue growth". After Lucent plummeted on the stock market, and the workforce was reduced to 20%, Lucent merged with Alcatel in 2006. However, things did not improve. Although not following McGinn's practice, in December 2010 Alcatel-Lucent was found guilty of paying bribes to foreign government officials to illegally win business in Latin America and Asia[21] and agreed to pay more than US$137 million to settle charges brought against it by the federal government. Setting targets that are beyond what your people and processes can deliver thus brings you even closer to these disastrous consequences.

The third type of bad practice connected to targets is the one displayed by employees when the phenomenon of "storming" occurs. Back in 1956, Joseph Berliner wrote an article entitled "A problem in Soviet business management"[22] where he examined the diffused practice in Soviet firms to rush to meet production quotas at the end of every month, which created quality and equipment maintenance problems.[10] Over half a century later this problem still occurs and in pretty much all organizations. The technical word for it is "budgeting". This story could probably be recounted by many of you reading this book.

Let us take any manufacturing firm in which the top management is struggling to achieve quarterly sales targets: this is often not only a problem for the firm, but it also poses a serious threat to top managers' bonuses. Three months before the end of the financial year it is decided that product prices will increase on the first day of the following financial year. This produces the effect of customer orders rushing in to take advantage of the "last opportunity sale". Similar to our previous cases, this decision is not at all related to competition or increases in product quality; rather it is due to two simple reasons: the desire to receive a bonus at the end of the year and a desire to lower expectations for the ensuing financial cycle.[9] Sadly, such a disconnect between employees and customers does not happen only when targets are too high, but also when they are too low: a salesperson, after meeting his monthly sales target, may decide to spend the rest of the month playing golf rather than working on new sales leads.[5]

Related to "storming" is the phenomenon of "sweep weeks" experienced by English public healthcare organizations during most of the 2000s. For the purposes of compiling league tables of hospitals, as discussed in the previous chapter, it was decided that the performance of the hospitals was to be measured only during specific weeks in order to be fair to everyone. It is no wonder then that A&E wait-time performance increased dramatically during these "sweep weeks" relative to the previous weeks and months. Figure 6.1 shows the average wait-time performance for all hospitals in England in the weeks before and during the one-week measurement period. In the month before the "sweep week", the mean percentage of patients treated within four hours was 85%; during the "sweep week", it was 93%.

Concerned that A&E departments were faking improvements in their wait times, the British Medical Association carried out a survey of 500 A&E consultants and found that 56% of hospitals hired extra doctors and nurses for the seven days in which they knew they would be assessed. In addition, a quarter required staff to work double or extended shifts and 14% cancelled routine surgery to free up beds to relieve the bottlenecks in A&E. Most consultants thought wrong clinical decisions were made as a result of the exercise. In addition, the *Guardian* newspaper accused the government of conniving in the scam by announcing the week in advance so as to persuade the public that it was achieving its political targets.[23]

The fourth concern over the use of performance targets is the so-called "ratchet effect". A good example of this perverse behaviour comes from the Moscow office of an international company. At this company, as in many, next year sales targets were formed on the basis of the current year figures, normally using the simple formula of "current year

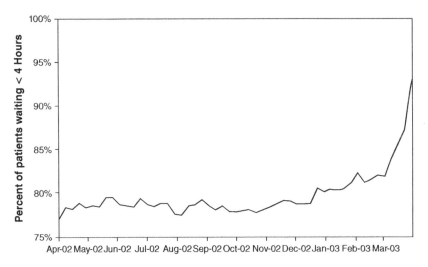

Figure 6.1 A&E wait times.[24]

sales + 25%". The target for 2010 was €1,000,000. When sales surpassed this figure by the September and the orders were still coming in thick and fast, the director of the Moscow office began the process of holding the orders until year end. By doing this, not only did he ensure a bonus for exceeding the target, but also effectively reduced the target for 2011 because of the backlog of orders. Therefore, when a target is expressed as an incremental advance over the previous year's results, it can cause managers to restrict performance to well below their potential.

Finally, in relation to the above story, another type of perverse behaviour can be described by the "threshold effect". Again, this is extremely pertinent to a sales situation. Imagine a scenario whereby all of the sales executives are given exactly the same target of selling £500,000 of merchandise. Everyone is incentivized in exactly the same way so as not to induce the earlier example of competition. However, now the problem arises that, as soon as the "threshold" is reached, no further effort is required, as the bonus has been secured. Therefore, no incentive for excellence is given, and the system of targets may result in an actual decrease in performance.

Table 6.1 reports the main problems with target setting we have outlined in this section. One way to consider them would be to dismiss them as unique occurrences, which cannot be generalized. The argument therefore could be that target setting is by and large useful and beneficial, but sometimes it may have unintended consequences. Another way to view targets would be to regard the reported issues as standard, and therefore dismiss target setting as the "wrong thing to do" and assume that it will necessarily lead to worse performance.[25] If we adopted the first stance then we would not be able to explain why certain issues occur; if we adopted the second, we would then be generalizing from a few specific cases, which would not necessarily give us a good rule to follow. Our perspective is, therefore, that target setting can be beneficial, but that it has to be done with care and with sufficient understanding of the main issues involved.

Table 6.1   Main issues with target setting.

Problems	Likely consequences
Targets used as control mechanisms	Targets, rather than underlying aims and objectives, become the focus of attention; fear and low morale.
Overly challenging targets	Data manipulation; unhealthy internal competition; unethical behaviours; alternatively, apathy and withdrawal.
"Storming" – concentrating efforts to achieve targets at a specific point in time	Abrupt, unsustainable improvements; underperformance; damaged processes and equipment during the "storm periods".
"Ratchet effect", because of incremental increases to current targets	Decrease in overall results; underexploited opportunities.
"Threshold effect", because of uniform output targets	The target (threshold) is reached, but nothing more; underexploited opportunities; loss of high performers.

WHEN TARGETS DO GOOD

The first thing to consider when developing targets is to understand which type of target you are introducing. For some people, targets like

100% completion of a task on time, zero defects or 100% customer satisfaction are good targets as they are challenging and aspirational, and they push people to achieve more. For others, targets have to be grounded in previous data so that they are realistic. For others yet again, targets are set as thresholds; something to be ensured. None of these perspectives are correct or incorrect. The point is that, when you set targets, you have to be aware that different types exist and that they will be more or less suitable depending on the context and the way they are managed.[26]

Aspirational targets can be extremely powerful when linked to a continuous improvement approach. The strive for perfection makes complete sense in the presence of feedback loops and within a culture that supports innovation and does not blame failure on teams, departments or, more importantly, individuals. A well-known type of aspirational target is a so-called "zero tolerance" or "zero defects" target. In this case, there is an absolute importance of preventing something from happening. Targets like this are often found in high-reliability organizations, such as nuclear power stations or in the prison service, where a target of zero breakouts by dangerous prisoners is certainly something to aspire to.

In general, it is good practice to set performance targets on the basis of previous performance and, if possible, when you have sufficient knowledge of your processes and the key sources of variation in your performance. Importantly, we may decide *not* to set targets until the statistical properties and sources of variation of a process or activity are adequately understood. In this case, the role of measurement might be confined to monitoring until drivers of improvement are identified. A good example of this is the monitoring of bovine spongiform encephalopathy (BSE), or mad cow disease, cases in the early 2000s. Even though this was a critical situation that needed to be acted upon, post-mortem examinations of cattle, which were mandatorily slaughtered in the European Union, took over six months. A tighter target on timings could have reduced that period; however, great insight was gained through this initiative. Indeed, thanks to the results of the examinations, sources of variation and potential process improvements became much clearer.[27] Therefore, the achievement of a target will often depend on the current, and possibly future, processes and our ability to affect the sources of variation.

Although targets can be used for different reasons, it is also important to pay attention to how targets are framed. Prevention or control-oriented targets, such as zero defects, may generate vigilance but also a negative emotion in employees, whereas promotion or growth-oriented targets may foster eagerness and positive emotions. This point takes us further into the behavioural effects of target setting.

CLARITY AND COMMITMENT

A major factor that influences the attainment of targets is people's understanding of the target itself. In this context, goal clarity means that an individual's perception of the specificity, rather than the vagueness, of the target to be achieved has a positive effect on a person's subsequent motivation and effort. Moreover, if people commit to a specified level of performance, psychologically they will be more inclined to achieve the target. In particular, the target should be not only understood but also negotiated, so that the employee has some input into its setting. This is often referred to as "goal commitment". Research has shown that, if such a dialectical process is not followed and targets are imposed on employees, goal commitment will be considerably lower.

As well as undertaking what needs to be achieved, an individual or team has to be clear about the role they will play in the achievement of the target. "Role clarity" describes the understanding an individual has about the expectations and behaviours associated with his or her work role. In other words, if I know what the target is, but I'm not sure about what it is that I have to do to hit it, my performance will not be optimal. Therefore, targets and objectives not only need to be clearly stated and well defined, but the individual needs to be equally clear about how to perform his or her job.[28]

When tasks are sufficiently easy and the work fairly repetitive, setting targets can be very beneficial, as goal clarity and role clarity are naturally high. For example, the American Pulpwood Association found that target setting led to significant increases in the productivity of loggers.[19] Pulpwood crews were matched and assigned to either an experimental target setting group or a control group. The saw hands were given a tally meter to keep track of the number of trees they cut down. The crews with a specific challenging target immediately outperformed those in the control group. The assignment of targets resulted in these workers seeing their work as challenging and meaningful, and job attendance grew considerably, as the employees began to take pride in comparing their performance relative to the target. These same crew members left work each day with a sense of accomplishment and a sense of personal effectiveness as a result of hitting the target.

However, in situations of higher uncertainty, such as in periods of deep change and transition, goal clarity, goal commitment and role clarity deserve even greater attention. Take the case of a large American company that produces, sells and installs a wide variety of home improvement and building products to large retailers such as Home Depot, Lowes and Menards, and to wholesale accounts consisting mainly of large-scale home builders and installation contractors.[29] In both of these segments, consolidation of the market has resulted in a situation where the company sells primarily to very large customers. During the 1990s, top management opted for a strategy of cost leadership, based primarily on process management. Lean thinking practices and procedures were introduced throughout the firm and progressively became part of the overall culture. However, by the mid-2000s, this strategy began to yield diminishing returns: low-cost suppliers, mainly located in China, were making it increasingly hard to compete purely on price. This situation prompted a shift in strategy from cost leadership to product differentiation through the use of radical innovation. In order to track progress, a performance indicator, measuring the percentage of sales derived from new products, was introduced. This appears, at face value, to be eminently sensible: if you want to promote innovation, you may measure the relative weight of new products, in terms of sales, income and profit, and often introduce additional targets to further align employees' behaviour to the new strategy. However, in this case no information was provided on how the target was to be achieved.

Under the previous strategy, the "how" was clear thanks to the systematic effort of introducing a certain way of working, and of communicating what was acceptable and what was not. However, through the change in strategy, confusion arose over the new "how". Indeed, a lack of "role clarity" had three main repercussions: firstly, despite changes in rhetoric and communications, behaviours remained pretty much the same, as employees were still behaving according to the previous paradigm, attempting to reduce waste and controlling cost rather than trying to come up with radically new ideas. Secondly, the performance indicator and the target were gamed, as newly introduced products were often slightly modified versions of existing ones. Thirdly, because of these difficulties, many employees began to challenge the very idea of pursuing the new strategy, thus demonstrating increasingly lower goal commitment. If, instead, goal clarity and goal commitment had been better aligned with role clarity, the transition from one way of working to the other would most likely have been more successful.

Similar conclusions were drawn in a recent study of target setting in a sales environment. Two of our colleagues found that when sales people have a clear idea of their role and of the performance expectations, and when they have participated in the target setting process, they are more likely to perceive their targets as less difficult.[3]

It is worth noting that, although in the example of the home improvement company reported above, the performance measurement system acted as a barrier to change, it could have actually played the opposite role. Indeed, it could have enabled change by providing information about the organization's new strategy and operations, and clarity over the employees' roles within the organization, their understanding of the main drivers of performance and the effect of their actions on the attainment of corporate objectives, had it been applied correctly.

UNEXPECTED BENEFITS

Whilst the careful design and implementation of performance targets can lead to planned positive outcomes, we have also come across numerous examples of unexpected positive effects. A typical use of targets is their implementation in individual performance appraisals. Several studies have shown that in these cases the use of targets has generated performance improvements, but not necessarily because of increased individual motivation, rather because the process of setting targets led to more frequent and focused dialogue between managers and employees. As an American civil servant put it: "We had lots of negotiation between heads of our programs and the [Office of Management and Budget] about how ambitious the targets should be. It is not our goal in life to come to work to fail. We want goals we can get to and not stretch goals or pie-in-the-sky goals."[30] So, it is not the simple fact of having a target, or the financial rewards attached to it, which has a beneficial impact on performance; rather, the introduction of the target can trigger a discussion over how employees could perform better. Conversely, we could argue that many of the failures attributed to targets are not due to the tools called targets, but rather to a lack of dialogue and feedback within organizations.

Another interesting example of unexpected positive consequences is so-called "complementarity". Essentially, sometimes improvement in one area does not happen thanks to indicators and targets related to it, but to indicators and targets introduced in other areas. For example, the creation of a stable and task-directed classroom environment, which aids teaching topics for standardized tests, can promote classroom learning in general. Complementarity is also created when the achievement of the target is accompanied by business process redesign. In the case of the English healthcare system, the introduction of the four-hour waiting target in A&E led to the introduction of two new processes: "see and treat", which proposed the redesign of traditional triage procedures so as to treat minor injuries more quickly, and "wait for a bed", which produced a better scheduling of inpatient operations and releases.[10] Although complementarity can be relevant and beneficial, its opposite, "effort substitution", must be taken into account whenever considering the introduction of targets, and, in this case, its unexpected negative consequences. In the case of A&E departments, improvements in speed could, for example, lead to decreases in quality or to optimizing performance in local areas without considering the bigger picture: for example, patients are seen quickly in A&E, but then have to wait longer in the other wards.

LEARNING POINTS

In this chapter, we have seen examples of absurd and dysfunctional behaviours, and outright unethical decisions made by individuals and teams to achieve performance targets. In some instances, targets created a disconnection between employees and customers, unhealthy competition within the organization and excessive risk-taking. In other cases, data was manipulated, monthly production quotas were met at the expense of the overall business, and unsustainable peaks in performance were achieved in "sweep weeks". Also, incremental targets were found to restrict performance to well below the potential of an organization, and the introduction of the same target to all units in a system resulted in an actual decrease in performance by top performers.

On the flip side, we have discussed equally compelling research evidence that advocates the use of performance targets. We have shown you that if a target is appropriately designed and the person, or group of people, is committed to it, that the individual or team has sufficient ability and resources to achieve it, and they are not subject to other conflicting targets, there is a positive relationship between target difficulty and task performance.[31] However, the design and implementation of targets also entail a series of choices, as laid out in Table 6.2.

Table 6.2   Main choices when introducing performance targets.

Choices	Options
Try to do the same better or to do something different?	Performance targets or learning targets
What type of target?	Aspirational, process-based or threshold
How many?	Few to ensure focus; many to avoid target fixation
Modify an existing target?	Yes, to reflect changes in the organization and its environment. No, to maintain consistency and capture trends
What timescale?	Shorter term, to be more accurate; longer term, to provide a wider perspective and stimulate investments

Let us take now take each of these points to show you how best to reap the benefits of target setting.

Types of targets

The first aspect of target setting you should take into account relates to the main aim of introducing the target: do you want to be better at doing the same thing, or do you want to do things differently? Recent research has made a distinction between these two types of objectives by labelling them "performance targets" and "learning targets". The former is typically framed in such a way that attention is predominantly on improving performance; for example, "reduce energy consumption by 5% this quarter". This target is clear and fairly straightforward. However, if you focus too narrowly on a performance target, you may be dissuaded from finding alternative solutions or methods to help you learn how to perform the task differently and/or more effectively.

If, instead, the objective of "reducing energy consumption" encompasses some form of knowledge or skill acquisition, rather than just effort or persistence, it will be more appropriate for you to focus on the discovery of effective task processes. The target may still be to "reduce energy consumption by 5% this quarter", but you should also allocate sufficient time and resources for your employees to propose, say, "three effective strategies to decrease energy consumption". In other words, instead of agreeing a performance target and acting immediately, learning targets usually entail periods in which alternatives are trialled and more frequent discussions take place between managers and employees. As some of the anecdotes above have demonstrated, setting specific, challenging performance targets is not likely to be prudent in situations that are uncertain or where great improvements are demanded.[16] Therefore, if you do decide to set a target, you should also consider whether the focus is on what to achieve or how to achieve it.

In addition, when choosing which type of target to use, be aware of the fact that what may initially be aspirational can quickly be disregarded. Earlier we discussed the positive use of zero tolerance targets, which in certain situations are essential. However, remember that when extreme-value or threshold targets are set and cannot be met, as with the infamous "no patient shall wait in accident and emergency (A&E) for more than four hours", they can lead to the somewhat paradoxical result that the target quickly becomes irrelevant: as soon as one patient has waited longer than four hours, the target is no longer viable and is therefore discarded. Furthermore, extreme-value targets may involve the utilization of disproportionate resources to prevent negative occurrences, so it is important to carefully assess the use of such targets from a cost/benefit point of view. In the given example, "95% of patients wait in A&E for less than four hours" is a more cost-efficient and continuously relevant target.[27]

An important question to ask when designing a target is whether it will focus attention on the right thing (more on this in Chapter 8). If you use a target to direct an individual's attention towards actions that are related to the target, then be careful that this is not at the expense of what is equally important but not relevant for the attainment of this target. Targets can function like blinkers and if a target is too specific and narrow, everything else suddenly disappears. A typical example is "teaching to the test" in education: if the only thing that matters is the final score in a test, the teachers will focus only on what will be examined, and the students will make sure that they learn all possible answers to all possible questions by heart, not really caring to understand the reasons for such answers. One way to overcome target and measurement fixation is to introduce more targets so as to reflect the complexity of the tasks at hand. However, this is not without its problems, as too many targets often result in confusion over organizational and individual priorities. Also, if you have several targets, it is quite likely that you will try to achieve the easiest ones. Unfortunately, this may not be very useful for the organization!

Setting targets

Once you have decided on the type of target you wish to set, and the behaviour you wish to drive, you then need to set a value for the target. In addition to the pointers made throughout this chapter, it is worth making two further remarks on the mechanics of target setting. Firstly, performance improvements are rarely linear or incremental; rather, they happen in steps, sometimes thanks to a redesign or transformation of services and processes. Therefore, it is not very smart to progressively sharpen targets and expect performance to follow a specific trajectory of improvement year on year. Rather, targets should be re-examined and set following changes in context. A nice illustration of this is the world high jump record. Prior to 1912 competitors in the high jump were not allowed to run up to the bar, they could only do a standing jump.

The record, set in 1900, remained at 1.65 m for 12 years. Once a change in process was made, allowing jumpers to run up to the bar, the male world record was increased to 2.00 m. After World War II, American and Soviet athletes started to develop a new technique, the straddle. This different approach would endure until the late 1970s and push the male record to 2.35 m. However, in the 1960s, with the introduction of soft crash mats, the American athlete Dick Fosbury pioneered what has now become the most commonly used technique, the Fosbury Flop. Thanks to this method, further records could be established, bringing the male world record to 2.45 m. Therefore, when setting a target you need to ensure that it is achievable given the current situation, or whether changes in resources, market conditions or in organizational processes should take place first. It would have made no sense to set a target for the high jump record to 2.45 m with early 20th century rules.

Secondly, the time frame of targets should be carefully assessed. Long-term targets may be problematic in turbulent, unstable environments: demand may suddenly increase, new competitors may enter the market, and new policies may be introduced. Also, long-term targets can be problematic as they may be inaccurate, which will in turn lead to some of the perverse consequences we outlined in this chapter, such as the ratchet and threshold effects. These points make a strong argument for setting targets whose time span is sufficiently short. However, short-term targets can be problematic too, as in the case of quarterly financial targets, which can contribute to the well-known and dreaded pursuit of short-term gains, often at the expense of long-term success or stability. Therefore, it is very important to consider each case in its own merits and strike a balance between short- and long-term targets.

Feedback

Once targets have been agreed, it is necessary to have regular discussions and feedback with those who are attempting to achieve them. The process of setting a target is fundamental in providing clarity over priorities and expectations, whereas dialogue and feedback are necessary in ensuring that productive efforts towards achieving the target are sustained. Moreover, research has shown that most of the added value provided by targets stems from the collective discussion and learning arising during their construction and subsequent reviews. Importantly, though, reviews should focus on the factors that led to a success or failure, rather than on the mere monitoring of deviations from preset levels of performance.[32]

Similarly, a review of performance appraisals and merit pay concluded that the interaction between the manager and the employee, whilst setting and reviewing targets, can increase an employee's commitment and understanding of targets and feelings of trust towards the management. From this point of view, training both managers and employees in how to set targets during performance appraisals, and how to provide feedback, would certainly be beneficial.[33]

Targets and incentives

Although in this chapter we have not examined in detail the links between performance targets and incentives, many of the anecdotes that have described poor, bad or distinctly criminal behaviour exist because an individual or an organization would have profited from meeting the target (more on this in Chapter 9). However, if targets are used to incentivize better performance, it is worth considering how best to combine them with bonuses. Table 6.3 demonstrates how each method has its pros and cons, and suggests ways of avoiding these pitfalls.

In summary

Each of the above learning points will still have inconsistencies and pitfalls associated with them. However, we believe that if you consider these five key points, whenever you introduce a target, you should be able to avoid some of the measurement madness described herein:

1. Not all targets are self-evident: explicit communication should be aimed at clarifying why you are introducing targets, what kind of targets you are using, what they mean, and how they relate to the organization's objectives.
2. Targets must be discussed and agreed with the people that are going to be accountable for reaching them, even if they have been set centrally.
3. All targets must be clearly communicated alongside an agreed action plan designed to reach them.

Table 6.3 Combinations of performance targets and bonuses [34]

Methods	Pros	Cons	Mitigation of negative effects
Stretch targets with bonuses for success	Strong incentive; it leaves no ambiguity about what is required	Temptation to think short range, take shortcuts and cheat	Set rules of conduct; leaders as role models; clear vision
Multiple target levels with multiple bonus levels	Less temptation to shortcut or cheat; highly competent employees who just miss a high-level target still get rewarded	Less motivation to try for the highest level	Set minimum level (standard) below which performance is considered inadequate
Linear/continuous bonus system	No "loss" for getting close to a higher target level and just missing it; an employee gets paid for exactly what is achieved. No upper limit to the bonus. Less temptation to cheat or take shortcuts	Difficult to calculate. Less pressure for the employee to "stretch". Often impossible to guarantee unlimited compensation	Set minimum level (standard) below which performance is considered inadequate
Motivate by targets but pay for performance. Specific, challenging targets are given, but the decision about bonus awards is made after the fact so as to take account of the full context in which the target is pursued	Flexibility and comprehensiveness	The boss should be knowledgeable about the full context and also try to minimize favouritism or bias	Good and transparent leadership; good information flows

4. From an organizational point of view, targets will be more effective if the leadership is supportive; a clear vision for the organization exists; feedback and recognition are provided; failure to attain the target will not necessarily lead to individual blame; and individuals and teams are sufficiently trained to achieve the targets.
5. Targets should be: neither too high nor too low; allocated appropriately across individuals and teams; consistent with each other and with the organization's strategy; based on rigorous data analysis that takes into consideration more than just past performance; and periodically reviewed.

AND FINALLY...

We have seen throughout this chapter that targets can help align behaviours, motivate employees and improve organizational performance. Advocates of targets also argue that, if desired levels of performance are not specified, we would be left with "do your best" encouragements, which are too abstract and vague. Not providing a clear external reference for evaluation and simply saying "do your best" would allow for a wide range of performance levels that are acceptable to different people.[35]

However, even after following all of our recommendations, setting purely outcome-driven targets can make normally sane individuals behave in the most insane ways. So we leave you with this reminder of what can happen if you set the target wrong...

A train company, concerned with arrival times because the regulator would fine them for persistent lateness, set a target for their drivers to arrive at the destination within five minutes of the publicized timetable. Given that the target was a final outcome target, if a train was running late, the driver would simply not stop at any of the intermediate stations, leaving passengers on board and those awaiting the train completely stranded!

7

Gaming and Cheating

The managing director of a small pharmaceuticals company in Russia was determined to combat the endemic tardiness of his employees. He considered a number of ways of doing this, even incentivizing his workers financially, just for turning up on time. However, eventually he decided that his best course of action was to punish his staff for their lateness. Therefore, he introduced a system of fines whereby an employee would be fined the equivalent of $1 for every minute he or she was late. So, if an employee was ten minutes late, an equivalent of ten US dollars was deducted from their monthly pay cheque. The information on who was on time was easily collectable, as the workers had to "swipe in" using magnetic cards. After the system was implemented, the records showed that the managing director was now achieving perfect punctuality, although productivity did not seem to be improving. A closer examination of the behaviour of the workforce showed that the majority of them did show up at 09:00 sharp or slightly earlier, but then proceeded to have breakfast, drink coffee, do their makeup and check their bank balances on the Internet – all using the company's resources. Those who did not want to get out of bed earlier, however, came up with a new and much more elaborate solution – their swipe cards would be given to a designated person, who was rotated and who would show up on time to swipe the whole stack of cards through the entrance scanner before 09:00. The sleepier of the employees would then arrive as usual, and the real work would not start until after 09:30. Interestingly, the manager only became aware of this "strategy" when someone tried to "swipe" 12 people into an elevator that was built to hold only 10 persons.

If we look at this example more closely, we can see that, although this policy clearly backfired, it did so in two distinctly different ways. In the first instance, where the employees arrived on time but then proceeded with their personal administration, they only made the smallest and easiest possible adjustment to their behaviour, with the overarching aim of maintaining the existing order of things. In the second instance, however, the employees used the new measure actively, creating a new and more elaborate scenario involving a new pattern of behaviour. This helped them make use of and even abuse the measure for their own purposes. It is this secondly, active and often detrimental response that is a major pitfall in the use of performance measurement, and this is what we call "gaming".

Flipping through the pages of this book, you will have seen that gaming is a persistent theme in the discussions on performance measurement and is a particular form of measurement madness. In our opening story of Mike's Performance Excellence meeting, the directors had become opposed to the use of measures, targets and rewards, because they were repeatedly observing instances of dysfunctional behaviours. In particular, they felt that employees were "gaming" the system, exploiting it for their own advantage to the detriment of the company's overall performance. Our discussions thus far on comparisons, target setting and conflicting measures have already brought up examples of gaming. Given its common occurrence and distinct nature, we have therefore decided to dedicate a separate chapter to its analysis. We will look at this phenomenon in depth and will separate it from other types of response to measurement; analyze its relationship to cheating; discuss the different types of gaming and their effects; and finally examine some of the ways of dealing with it and mitigating its effects.

GAMING: WHAT IS IT?

After a long transatlantic flight, with little sleep and airline food as the only nourishment in eight hours, the one thing that every traveller craves is to get through the airport as quickly as possible, to get home for a hot shower and a proper meal. Delays at immigration are understandable, but waiting alongside the slow, mechanical progression of the luggage carousel as a lone case passes by for the third time only adds to the interminable, mind numbing boredom that is a part of world travel. However, it is not only the weary traveller who wants his passage through the airport to go smoothly and quickly; this is also the wish of the airport authorities. One of the most infamous examples of gaming in the field of performance measurement is the story of improving the luggage handling system at one of the UK's major international airports.[1] In order to try to improve the flow of passengers through the airport, the management decided to focus on reducing the time that travellers spent waiting in the baggage reclaim hall for their possessions. The executives therefore authorized the design and implementation of a performance indicator to measure the time between the moment the plane landed and the time the *first* piece of luggage hit the carousel belt. It was felt that this measure was appropriate, because it would be unfair to compare the overall time it takes to deliver all bags, if you are offloading an Airbus 380 or a Boeing 737. This performance measure was used to monitor the work of baggage handlers in the hope that their performance would result in the faster flow of passengers through the terminal.

The weeks following the introduction of the new performance measure showed a steady improvement in the performance of the baggage handling teams and produced a consistent record of achieving the target. However, the level of customer complaints regarding the delays to the arrival of their luggage increased, and this therefore forced the management to investigate the process behind the results. What the executives discovered was that when a plane landed, the baggage handling team met it as quickly as possible, selected a light, medium-sized bag and gave it to the fittest member of the team. The handler then hurried to the terminal and placed the bag on the carousel – target met! Meanwhile, the rest of the team unloaded the plane at their leisure and proceeded, with no particular haste, to take the baggage to the terminal.

Given the large volume of stories and examples of gaming, it may come as a surprise to you that, in the vast collection of writings on performance measurement and management, there is no common definition of gaming, even though it is a common side effect of measurement. We have therefore created our own definition based on our experience and research in the field. We define gaming as:

> a *response* to performance measurement that involves the development of *a new and stable pattern of behaviour* that aims to take advantage of the measure in a way that is (1) *different* from the original purpose of the measure; (2) resulting in an *improvement* in the measured aspect of performance; but (3) *detrimental* for the actual performance.

The example of the baggage handlers demonstrates how, following the introduction of the new performance indicator, the *response* of the teams was to develop a completely *new, elaborate, and stable pattern of behaviour* in order to game the measure. Their response was not simply to speed up the delivery of the baggage to the carousel, as was hoped for by the management team; rather, they devised a relatively sophisticated way of taking advantage of the measure that was *different* from the original purpose. And what about the hoped-for performance improvement? Well, as per our definition of gaming, the recorded data did show a marked improvement, but one which was *detrimental* to the flow of passengers through the airport. Not only did travellers wait for a longer time, but the customers standing at the belt were becoming ever more frustrated – and envious of the lucky person whose bag had been delivered.

In our earlier chapter on targets we discussed at length the issue of the four-hour waiting target in A&E in the English National Health Service. The *response* of the administrators and clinicians was to introduce newly devised arrangements, where a number of patients were moved across a dividing line into something called a "clinical decision unit", thereby removing them from A&E and its target. This became such a *stable pattern of behaviour* that it was replicated in other hospitals across the country. The Department of Health's hoped-for outcome was that patients would be treated more swiftly; however, although the creation of a CDU did cut the waiting times in A&E, patients' treatment was still a drawn-out process. As the Mid Staffordshire example demonstrated, the gaming of the target was actually *detrimental* to people's lives.

As we have repeatedly seen in this book, measurement will almost always change people's behaviour; however, not all such changes are of equal severity. Some measures will provoke relatively minor adjustments, which can often be predicted and the associated risks mitigated, and which will not necessarily result in a worsening performance. Gaming, however, always involves a major, purposeful change in behaviour, whose nature and shape may be quite difficult to predict and whose impact on performance is almost always detrimental. Unlike in a situation where minor adjustments take place simply to avoid the consequences of the new measure, gaming requires the participant to have a thorough understanding of the performance measure and to make a conscious and elaborate response to it, as they did in the Russian company by getting one person to swipe in whole groups of colleagues. Bearing this distinction in mind, let us take a closer look at the elements of gaming in comparison to the less significant responses to the pressures of performance measurement, as outlined in Table 7.1.

Table 7.1   Behavioural responses to gaming.

	Minor response	**Gaming**
Extent of change	Minor adjustment	Major change
Nature change	An adjustment in the existing behavioural pattern	A new and stable behavioural pattern; a new scenario
Underlying aim	Maintaining the existing order; the smallest change possible; inertia	Actively taking advantage of the performance indicator to improve the reported results without necessarily changing the true performance
Predictability	What might change is easy to predict	What might change is difficult to predict
Effect on performance	Usually minor; can be either positive or negative	Usually major and usually negative

Table 7.1 shows that gaming always refers to a major and elaborate change in behaviour whose aim is to take advantage of the performance indicator and use it for purposes other than those for which it was originally intended. As such, the shape of the gaming response is difficult to predict and usually has a detrimental effect on performance.

For instance, in the previous chapter, we talked about the situation when train drivers, acting under the pressure of on-time arrival targets, would simply skip intermediate stops en route to their final destination where the "target clock" would stop. This is an immediate and perhaps predictable response to performance pressure. A more elaborate gaming scenario, which comes from the same railroad, was the decision of the network managers to hold up trains that were "almost late" in order to give way to other trains behind them. This way, the managers ensured that the target was met for the majority of the services, whilst the performance of a few trains, and their unlucky passengers, dramatically moved from "almost late" to "hopelessly late".

Gaming responses to performance measurement can take many different forms, so understanding these generic forms may make it easier to spot a developing gaming situation and therefore be able to identify an appropriate response. Before we turn to a discussion of the types of gaming, let us look at those situations where both minor responses and major gaming scenarios can acquire darker undertones and transform into cheating.

GAMING AND CHEATING

Every year, millions of individuals around the world are required to complete their tax returns. Unfortunately, in many jurisdictions the rules have become ever more complicated, and governments have designed multiple incentive schemes for people to reduce their tax liabilities, such as saving in pension schemes or investing in new and potentially profitable start-up companies. During the recession of the late 2000s, Western governments had to tighten their belts as well as maximize the collection of tax monies. Whilst scrutinizing schemes that enabled individuals to avoid certain tax duties, Her Majesty's Revenue and Customs (HMRC), the UK's ministry tasked with collecting taxes, unearthed a number of practices both at a corporate and at an individual level that they felt were closer to tax evasion than avoidance. It was found that a number of large global corporations were aggressively avoiding paying tax on their UK profits. For example, although Amazon had a UK operation, which employed 15,000 people and publicly reported a turnover of £207 million for 2011, their reported tax liability was only £1.8 million. Although not illegal, members of the UK Parliament sitting on the Public Accounts Committee accused Starbucks, Google and Amazon of "immorally" minimizing their UK tax bills.[2] On the other hand, several clever schemes were introduced to evade taxes altogether. For example, in January 2013, HMRC published the pictures of 32 criminals who had been sentenced to a combined total of 155 years and 10 months in prison. Those jailed included three "green fraudsters" who conducted a number of fictitious trades of European Union carbon emission allowances in order to reclaim £38m in value added tax.[3]

Understanding the difference between tax avoidance and tax evasion helps us comprehend the difference between gaming and cheating. Although these terms are often used interchangeably to describe the manipulation of performance information that takes place in response to measurement, this is not completely correct. Gaming refers to the creation of alternative ways of doing things, exhibiting new behavioural patterns, which satisfy the requirements of the measurement system and the corresponding targets, whilst not necessarily responding to the original intent of the measure. As such, gaming can be described as "exploiting the loopholes" or "working the system", as people often do when avoiding paying more tax than is absolutely necessary. Cheating, on the other hand, includes an ethical dimension and involves an active and deliberate misrepresentation of performance information, from internally defined procedures to national laws, as in the examples of Enron and Informix that we saw in Chapter 6. Such misrepresentation usually breaches explicit regulations and can be deemed illegal.

If you consider the baggage handling story, it has been reported that, at other airports, baggage teams became even more "creative" and purposefully used an old battered red suitcase to act as the first bag on the carousel, thus not even bothering to play the charade of unloading the plane. The red bag would be positioned near the uploading ramp of the carousel and placed on it some minutes after the arrival of the plane, after someone from the baggage team had pushed the button to start the carousel and hence register the moment at which the "time to deliver bags" clock would stop. This part of the baggage handlers' "solution" was bordering on cheating, as it was deliberately misrepresenting what was actually being achieved.

Of course, it is impossible to say with certainty where gaming ends and cheating begins. However, a continuum developed by two UK academics, Colin Fisher and Bernadette Downes,[4] may prove helpful in further distinguishing between the two terms. This continuum ranks various types of information manipulation ranging from the least dishonest, such as the selective presentation of information, to the more dishonest, such as downright distortion and fabrication of data. Gaming, defined similarly to the way we define it here, sits in the middle. If gaming is analogous to "working the system", it turns into cheating when the underlying quality of the information is manipulated, either to present a deliberate misrepresentation or, quite frankly, to tell a lie.[4] Let us take a look at some examples.

The Vehicle and Operator Services Agency (VOSA), a UK government agency responsible for the licensing and control of vehicles on the road, recently ran a campaign against falsifying tachograph records in commercial goods vehicles. Tachographs are devices that record the driver's activity, alongside the speed and distance travelled, and they alert the driver when a rest break is necessary. Such breaks are mandated by law to prevent a driver operating in a tired state. The use of tachographs was not seen favourably by drivers who, pushed by delivery deadlines and the pressure to complete orders, are often tempted to skip those breaks. Indeed, in 2010 there were 438 recorded cases of drivers using a magnet to falsify the tachograph reading, allowing them to drive longer distances without a break.[5] This is a clear example of cheating induced by the pressure to perform.

Cheating occurs equally in both the private and the public sector. For instance, a few years ago, Her Majesty's Courts Service, the branch of the UK's Ministry of Justice responsible for the operation of the country's courts, conducted an investigation into one of the country's magistrates' courts. The inquiry discovered that one of the court officials had advised her colleagues to misrepresent records in order to improve their reported performance. She suggested that court cases that had not been completed should be reclassified as "withdrawn" and removed from the system, thus improving the overall level of performance. The investigation concluded that, although the suggestion had been made, no action had been taken and no records had been altered.[34] This form of misrepresentation – reclassifying data in order to show an improvement in reported performance – is one of the most common forms of fraud committed with the aim of "performing to the measure".

Cheating is much more likely to occur where data is plentiful, complex and difficult to control, as is found in large organizations. The UK's National Health Service (NHS) is very complex, centrally governed and the fifth largest organization in the world.[6] In 2012, the NHS employed more than 1.7m people and had an annual operating budget of £106 billion. As the NHS has all of the attributes described, one could imagine it being a breeding ground for cheating. In the early 2000s, the UK government conducted a series of investigations into the operations of the NHS in England. The investigation revealed that, driven by the pressure to meet the national waiting lists targets, multiple hospitals had made inappropriate adjustments to patients' records. These adjustments ranged from recording false admission dates and quietly suspending patients from waiting lists, to amending waiting list reports and underrepresenting the number of long-waiting patients.[7] In Scotland, where waiting lists only applied to patients receiving inpatient treatment, hospitals reclassified people as outpatients when inpatient care had already been offered. The United States, with its high reliance on private medical care providers, is not exempt from cheating either, as the opportunity to misrepresent data is always tempting. For instance, "DRG Creep" is a well-documented practice, which refers to the reclassification of the treated condition into a more serious diagnosis-related group (DRG) in order to increase the cost of services, which in turn leads to higher reimbursements from the insurance companies.[8]

Similar practices can also be observed in the realm of education. The US experience with the Comprehensive Assessment Tests (CATs) in secondary education, which measure students' test scores in a number of subjects, demonstrates that pressure to perform drove schools to misrepresent the number of eligible students. For instance, according to the rules, students suffering from learning and other disabilities could be exempted from taking the Comprehensive Assessment Tests or from having their exam results included in the performance report. Whilst such practice could be considered appropriate, several academic studies have reported that many schools reclassified low-performing students as disabled or requiring special needs, thereby exempting them from being entered into the final report.[9] In 2013, the discovery of similar practices in the Atlanta Public Schools district not only produced a nationwide furore but also led to 65 teachers being indicted for manipulating the results of standardized tests in order to demonstrate schools' performance and secure federal funding.[10]

The same measure can, of course, engender both gaming and cheating behaviours. The opening story of being fined for being late included both gaming, as it involved a thorough understanding of the measure and creation of a new behavioural pattern to take advantage of it, and cheating, as employees essentially misrepresented the true time they showed up for work. Such instances are not rare, and a global survey of employee behaviour, conducted in 2011, showed that as many as 37% of UK respondents admitted to cheating when recording their work time, including asking someone else to swipe their card for them. The figure was somewhat lower in France and Canada but significantly higher in India, China and Australia.[11,12] Perhaps more worrying is the fact that the most recent US National Business Ethics Survey found that the majority of ethical violations (60%!) were committed by people in managerial positions.[13]

So, can cheating ever be eradicated? Can a performance measure be designed so that it does not induce people to misrepresent the numbers or lead to barefaced lying? Speaking on the BBC a few years ago, the President of the International Olympic Committee, Jacques Rogge, noted, "Drug-free sport in general is Utopia. It will be naive to believe that no-one will take drugs…Cheating is embedded in human nature."[14] If Rogge is correct, and the case of Lance Armstrong habitually cheating in the Tour de France[15] strengthens his argument, then hoping for a cheat-proof and game-proof performance measurement system may well be a utopian quest. However, if we want to reduce the likelihood of gaming and cheating, we should try to understand what factors increase the likelihood of people turning to these behaviours as a response. We also need to establish whether such responses fall into predictable categories and what we can do to mitigate this constant companion of measurement madness. Let us look at each of these issues in turn.

WHAT DRIVES GAMING AND CHEATING?

Why do people turn to gaming and cheating? Attempts to answer this question often lead to debates about the basic assumptions regarding human nature. Is cheating really embedded in human nature as Jacques Rogge suggested? And, if so, does that mean that we should expect people to take advantage of the system no matter what we do? Or, on the contrary, do we believe that, left to their own devices, people will take the initiative, exercise creativity, and strive to do their best to improve the performance of their organizations? How you answer these questions is very important, as your answers will influence the type of control system you will implement and the kind of management style you will adopt.

Academics have grappled with this tension for decades, and this has spawned numerous theories on how people behave and, therefore, how they could and should be managed. In 1960, Douglas McGregor introduced the distinction between Theory X and Theory Y, which encapsulated the difference in the assumptions made about human behaviour in organizations. Those managers who agree with Theory X assume that employees are inert, avoid responsibility and resist change, and, therefore, need to be managed by the use of rigid control systems. Instead, those who favour Theory Y consider people to be self-motivated, responsible, enjoy creative work and are open to change. Measurement systems are then utilized as guiding and enabling mechanisms, rather than monitoring and controlling ones. Moreover, the Theory X assumptions imply that employees would always look for ways to "beat the system" in an effort to do as little as possible. This is why we need to come up with more and more sophisticated measurement systems. From a Theory Y point of view, instead, people are seen as genuinely wanting to be better at what they do, and it is measurement systems themselves, when used as control mechanisms, that could actually end up causing dysfunctional behaviours.

More recently, in debates on employee motivation in the public services, another distinction known as "knights vs. knaves" has been proposed, which describes "knights" as those public servants who are believed to be motivated by the goal of creating value for society at large, and "knaves" as those whose motivation is driven by self-interest and personal gain.[16] Over the years these distinctions have become firmly embedded in management theory and have influenced thoughts about what we expect people to do and, consequently, how we approach the task of designing and using performance measurement systems. Other influences have been Agency Theory and Stewardship Theory. The former, with its focus on opportunistic go-getter behaviour, has underpinned virtually all thinking behind complex, target-driven compensation schemes and led to the explosion of the bonus culture (more on this in Chapter 9). Stewardship Theory, on the other hand, has tried to explain the persisting instances of altruistic behaviour in organizations and to draw managers' attention to nurturing and making productive use of the goodwill of employees.

None of these theories, however, have given us any conclusive explanations: it is impossible to make a sweeping but accurate statement about human nature. Also, context matters, and therefore any generalization may be inappropriate. While we cannot provide a definitive answer to the question of why people are driven to game or cheat, we can distil the factors that make gaming and cheating more or less likely to emerge. Looking at recent research and building on our experience, we can identify three very important contextual factors:

the pressure to perform, the type and intensity of performance targets imposed on the employees, and the organizational climate and culture in which people work.

The pressure to perform

In January 2014, the *New York Times* reported that the US Air Force had suspended 92 officers (out of about 200) at one of three bases that oversee the country's arsenal of intercontinental ballistic missiles.[17] Investigators found that, while undertaking monthly proficiency tests, missile launch officers were sent answers in text messages to their mobile phones. This soon became a cheating scandal; however, interestingly, the Air Force secretary, whilst not justifying the officers, spoke of a "climate of fear", which would have encouraged the officers to share test answers. Apparently, such a climate had been created not by the simple pressure to pass (90% was the pass mark), but by commanding officers' informal rule of not promoting any officer who did not score 100%. When 500 officers across the three bases were eventually retested, only 22 failed, and the average score was 95%. As the Air Force secretary stated, "the irony is that they didn't cheat to pass, they cheated to get 100 percent. This is not a healthy environment...."

The overwhelming pressure to perform is accountable for many instances of gaming and cheating. For example, upon investigating the manipulation of data in the NHS that we discussed earlier, the UK National Audit Office conceded that: "while this does not in any way excuse inappropriate adjustment...adjustments [to the data] were made in the context of pressure on Trusts and particularly Chief Executives to meet key departmental targets".[7] This theme runs as a red thread through almost every investigation of cheating-related incidents. The prosecutors in the Atlanta Public Schools scandal, mentioned earlier in the chapter, charged the superintendent with exerting "unreasonable pressure" on her staff in order to achieve the targets, as well as with creating an environment "where achieving the desired end result was more important than the students' education".[18] Similarly, with reference to the manipulation of crime figures by police officers in the UK that we discussed in Chapter 3, the Chief Constable reported that national performance targets "are still putting pressure on officers to do all they can to manipulate and create crime reductions. I don't think they do it because they are inherently corrupt, but because pressure is put down to reduce it."[19] Performance pressure drives people away from steady, sensible behaviour. Or, in the words of Warren Buffett, the legendary American investor, "managers that always promise to 'make the numbers' will at some point be tempted to *make up* the numbers".[20]

Pressure can, of course, come from sources other than performance targets, and can drive people to create very sophisticated gaming strategies. For instance, the BBC recently exposed a scam at one of London's colleges, which involved an elaborate gaming response to the pressure created by changing immigration regulations. Until early 2012, non-EU students completing their postgraduate degrees in the UK could apply for a two-year work visa, which entitled them to remain in the country. According to the new rules, instead, this entitlement was cancelled and a different system introduced, which did not have a work visa provision. In 2011, as the deadline for the abolishment of the original system was approaching, some staff at Rayat London College, a minor private institution that offered degrees validated by the University of Wales, created a system allowing students to sprint through their coursework in order to graduate early enough to apply for the work visa. The BBC was able to find evidence that the "gaming strategy" that was designed to exploit this situation included "an offer to hold examinations in which students can cheat in order to complete a 15-month qualification in under a week". Other elements of this strategy included coaching the students on how to navigate their way through the university exams and how to meet the requirements of the UK's immigration authority.[21] Following the investigation, the college went into liquidation.[22]

At this point, it is important that we remind ourselves that performance measurement is often introduced into organizations with the exact aim of altering behaviour. Therefore, behavioural consequences of measurement are not necessarily undesirable; indeed, measurement can provide greater clarity and focus on the organization's main aims and objectives. However, when measurement is used without considering the wider context in which people operate; without understanding the nature of the pressure that is being imposed on them; or, worse, with an explicit aim to control behaviour, the results are often exactly the opposite to what was expected. As the so-called Goodhart's law states, "Any observed statistical regularity will tend to collapse once pressure is placed on it for control purposes."[23] High pressure to perform and a narrow focus on control tend to produce precisely the gaming behaviours discussed thus far.

Targets – the wrong kind and in the wrong way

As we have seen, the pressure of measurement often takes the form of a performance target – the desired level of performance that we either set for ourselves or that is imposed on us from an external source. Given all the stories told in this chapter, one would expect targets to lead to gaming and cheating simply when they are set too high, but this is not necessarily so. The effect of performance targets on gaming and cheating is more nuanced, because it is not only the intensity but also *the kind* of pressure an individual is under that determines whether or not he or she is driven to play the system. In an experimental study, published in 2011, a team of researchers examined the effect of targets on cheating.[24] Similarly to the "performance targets" and "learning targets" mentioned in Chapter 6, these researchers distinguished between externally defined and personally set targets. Among the questions they asked were the following: does it matter whether the target is personally set or externally imposed? And, does the context play any role? The researchers discovered that the individuals with personally set targets demonstrated both a lower intention to cheat and fewer instances of actual cheating than individuals who were focused on the externally defined targets. Moreover, the latter's higher intention to cheat was evident across different contexts, for example work, sports and studies.

What is going on here? A couple of things: firstly, this and other studies show that cheating is not a personality trait; the world is not divided into "cheaters" and "honest citizens". Rather, the likelihood that a person will be drawn to gaming or cheating depends on the type of targets they want or have to achieve, and the ways in which those targets are set. This finding is supported by another piece of research where school children, who were transferred from learning target-oriented classes to performance target-oriented classes, showed an increase in cheating, because improving one's own competence was no longer of importance.[25] So, where gaming and cheating are concerned, there are no clear "knights or knaves".

What the study above also means for our discussion is that, although performance measurement undoubtedly puts pressure on people and as such may increase the likelihood of cheating and gaming, it actually matters how those targets are set and how the pressure is applied. If performance measurement is deployed with the aim of increasing employees' competence and allows people to use it in order to achieve personally meaningful goals, gaming is far less likely than if performance measurement is seen as an instrument of ensuring the achievement of an externally imposed standard. In other words, the way in which the pressure of measurement is applied matters at least as much as the intensity of such pressure.

The climate of competitiveness

Besides the intensity and the type of measurement pressure, the other key factor affecting the likelihood of gaming and cheating is the professional culture and climate in which a person operates. One research study showed that the likelihood of cheating was different in different contexts. As we have just seen, the individuals focusing on internally defined targets would always show a lower intention to cheat than the individuals focusing on externally defined ones. However, the overall level of cheating was highest in the educational setting, followed by work and then by sports. In other words, the context in which people would find themselves would affect how much they were prepared to game the system.

This finding shouldn't come as a surprise, as we all know that peer pressure and a climate of extreme competitiveness can drive people to do things that they would not do if the circumstances or the context were different. What is surprising, however, is how far-reaching this effect can be and in what contexts we can see this mechanism at play. Scientific research is a process of improving our understanding of the natural or social world around us. However, modern science is very complex and, despite myths of lone inventors and mad scientists, exemplary research is often undertaken by groups of people. Nonetheless, while teamwork is fundamental to scientific advances, this clashes with the fact that academic careers are based on individual output and personal contribution to a certain field of knowledge. Academia, as a professional field, is thus extremely competitive, with individuals vying for a place in the spotlight. Securing a place in that spotlight, however, works differently in the natural sciences as opposed to the social sciences. In the natural sciences, where teams of researchers working on the same problem but operating in different corners of the globe may discover the same answer, success is often a matter of being the first one to publish the solution. In the social sciences, however, there is frequently more than one valid answer to the same question and more than one angle from which to examine it fruitfully. Success, therefore, often depends on one's ability to stay in the spotlight longer and to persuade a larger audience that your answer is more useful or valid than others.

An interesting question then is this: given the intense competitive climate of the academic environment and the necessity to capture a large share of the audience, will social scientists be driven to cheat in order to advance their own output even though the spirit of academic research cries for collaboration? Given everything else that we have discussed in this chapter, you may expect the answer to this question to be "yes" – and you would be right!

A study conducted by Harvard Business School[26] looked at the way academics use the Social Science Research Network (SSRN), an online repository of research papers in social sciences. SSRN is one of the largest repositories available, and it allows researchers to submit papers for public access. Every time a paper is downloaded, SSRN registers it, creating the so-called "download count" for each paper. The papers with the highest number of downloads are shown in the "Top 10 List" within each discipline, thus giving the paper higher visibility and drawing the public's attention to it. Using an ingenious research design, the Harvard study examined whether the authors were downloading their own papers multiple times in order to artificially inflate the download count and make it to the coveted "Top 10 List".

The results demonstrated that the authors were indeed more likely to engage in downloading their own papers to increase the download count when they thought that had a fair chance of getting into the "Top 10 List". However, the most striking result of this research was that the gaming of the SSRN system through bogus downloads was most strongly driven by the authors' comparing themselves with their peers and trying to beat them in the download count. In other words, when academics saw their colleagues getting ahead in terms of SSRN downloads, they were more likely to start downloading their own papers to boost their count and close the gap![i]

---

[i] A revised version of this paper also shows that the more successful academics tend to *increase* self-downloads in order to maintain their status relative to their peers.

What this example shows is that a highly competitive culture will drive gaming behaviours to maximize output, even in contexts where fame and glory hinge on sharing and collaboration. The fact that this example comes from the field of scientific research is telling, because it shows yet again that cheating and gaming are not personality traits. Organizational culture, therefore, is one of the major determinants of such behaviour and one of the key factors to be considered when attempting to mitigate the gaming effects of performance measurement.

There are a couple of key messages that we would like you to take away from this discussion. Firstly, there is no evidence to suggest that people are inherently dishonest and inclined to game the system or, vice versa, that people are driven by altruism and a desire to help. Likewise, there is nothing to indicate that some people are drawn to the opportunity to cheat and others are immune to it. Rather, the likelihood that people will turn to gaming and cheating depends on the situational context in which they find themselves.

Secondly, the situational context is made up of three major components that affect people's inclination to try to game the system. The first factor to consider is that the propensity to game and cheat is directly proportional to the intensity of the pressure exerted by the performance measure. The higher the pressure, the more likely it is that people will feel compelled to engage in gaming behaviours in order to "make the numbers". The second consideration is that the way in which the pressure is exerted is just as important as its intensity. Achievement goals that are focused on hitting a certain level of performance and are the same for everyone are more likely to provoke gaming and cheating than goals that are competency based, developmental in nature and personally meaningful. And finally, the general culture and climate in an organization will have an effect on the likelihood of gaming and cheating. Organizations with a culture of extreme personal competitiveness, for instance, are far more likely to see instances of gaming than those with a more collaborative climate.

TYPES OF GAMING

As you know from experience, and as the examples in this chapter have illustrated, the list of specific gaming and cheating behaviours in organizations is endless. Behaviours range from intentionally mishandling data and interfering with its analysis to elaborate strategies that involve some serious planning. So how can you predict when these behaviours will be employed and how can you mitigate the consequences of these behaviours? It makes little sense to record every instance of gaming behaviour and then think through the implications and design appropriate remedies – the task would be too great. Therefore, it is far more useful to understand how gaming and cheating can be categorized in a way that would enable you to predict and effectively manage any potentially detrimental consequences.

There are several gaming typologies. One, for example, looks at the extent to which data manipulation results in changes to the actual performance. This allows individual instances of gaming to be put on a continuum from negligible changes in behaviour, to displaying supposed conformity to meeting the targets, to downright cheating.[29] Another typology couples the extent of gaming with whether its effects are internal to an organization or directed towards the outside world, allowing you to create a virtual map of where the effects of gaming are most felt.[27] Such typologies are useful, but very descriptive. In other words, they may help you to break down the list of gaming and cheating behaviours into manageable categories and to get a picture of what the current extent of gaming may be, but they are less helpful when you need to gauge the seriousness of potential gaming behaviours and you need to prepare to deal with their implications.

To overcome these deficiencies we have developed a typology that will enable you to diagnose the possible effects of cheating and gaming and estimate the seriousness of the intervention. In our opening story to this chapter, the Russian manager introduced a fine for employees coming into work late, and we saw that, unlike minor responses to performance measurement pressure, gaming involved a major change in behaviour that was difficult to predict. Therefore, the scope of behavioural change and the predictability of its shape and effect are important aspects in our typology.

The number and predictability of gaming behaviours

Figure 7.1 shows three levels of severity in gaming behaviours, ranging from changes in the way performance data are handled and processed, to the fabrication or intentional loss of data, to the creation of new

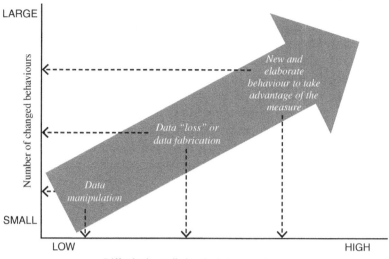

Figure 7.1   Severity of gaming behaviours.

and elaborate patterns of behaviour aimed at gaming the performance measure. The vertical axis shows you how many behaviours are likely to change given the severity of the gaming. The actual shape that these behaviours will take is sometimes easily predictable and sometimes less so, and your ability to predict the shape of the behavioural response depends very much on your knowledge of the organization: its people, culture, formal procedures and informal practices. The more dangerous the effects of gaming potentially are, the harder it will be for you to foresee exactly how the gaming response will play out in practice.

Let us have a closer look at the figure and the range of gaming behaviours it covers. The first two levels of gaming severity are concerned with changes made to data: this should come as no surprise, as a large proportion of performance management is based on collecting, analyzing and reporting performance data. However, the gravity of the response can be categorized differently depending on the extent to which performance data is distorted. The first level, data manipulation, is the least severe and can include such things as fiddling with the definitions of measures to boost or, conversely, reduce the measured output; selective disclosure of performance data; creative presentation of data; and the use of visualization techniques to conceal or distort the message. For example, one of the most common measures for public museums is the number of visitors, as most of them exist to make their collections accessible to a wide range of people.[28] Common sense would make us think that visitors are therefore those people who come to view the items and expositions. However, as research demonstrates, pushed by the pressure to make the numbers, some museums have redefined their performance measure, quietly and unofficially, to count as a visitor any person who enters the premises: officials, inspectors, contractors, even a lone dog.[27]

This is clearly an example of gaming as it leads to a new and stable pattern of behaviour engendered by the measure, but the number of behaviours that are changed is relatively small, because it is restricted to manipulating the data. Another example of data manipulation comes from the opening story of this book. During the Performance Excellence meeting, the sales director for Western Europe had put up a chart, which showed an incredible rise in sales. However, rather than being an actual major improvement, it was an instance of data manipulation whereby the y axis was not starting at zero, and, therefore, the pattern shown in the graph had been distorted. Although presenting a misleading picture, this is not an example of major behavioural change, nor of data fabrication; rather one of manipulation of existing data.

More often than not, data manipulation is a technical matter, and therefore it is often relatively easy to foresee the actual shape that the manipulation will take. As was mentioned earlier, the better you know your organization and the stronger your handle on the data management process, the easier it will be for you to predict what data is vulnerable to gaming and how that gaming might manifest itself. The general remedy lies in your comprehensive approach to data management, in your ability to ensure the quality of performance data and in your robust processes of data analysis and reporting.

Fabrication or intentional "loss" of data is the second level of severity. It differs from data manipulation in its greater number of gaming behaviours and consequently the gravity of their effects. Sometimes existing data is intentionally "lost" or "forgotten", as in the magistrates' court example, and sometimes data is created out of thin air. Unlike the case of data manipulation, where existing data is simply given an interpretive spin, in this case data is either erased or made up. This is where gaming begins to enter the territory that may be described as cheating or fraud, and thus its consequences are potentially far more serious. As this type of gaming behaviour often involves great creativity, the shape it will take is harder to predict than in the case of data manipulation, where no changes are made in the actual dataset. For instance, you may expect that if some data is "lost", it will not enter into the analysis. A good data management system, however, should enable you to detect and prevent this. On the other hand, predicting all the ways in which the results of the analysis may be fabricated is impossible. How should you deal with this then? At the end of the chapter, we provide a number of suggestions that you might consider.

Finally, "gaming proper" occurs when a response to performance measurement involves the creation of a new, elaborate and stable pattern of behaviour that is aimed at subverting the original intent of the performance measure. Whilst it is true that any gaming response will cause new behaviours to appear, sometimes such behaviours go beyond a change to simple routines and involve new and sophisticated scenarios that are aimed at gaming performance measures in ever more elaborate ways. Some of the earlier examples in this chapter have illustrated such situations: designating a person to swipe multiple cards at the morning check-in; physically drawing a line to split the A&E treatment room into multiple sectors; and reclassifying students to exempt them from taking national tests. This form of gaming has potentially the gravest consequences. Firstly, the more complex the new scenario is and the more people it involves, the more likely it is to stick and acquire its own momentum. It is far easier to fix a poorly defined measure than to make a team of A&E staff change their behaviour. Secondly, complex gaming strategies usually appear when people have thought about a performance measure and consciously decided to take advantage of it. Such a response is very difficult to reverse or even combat. Finally, elaborate gaming strategies divert resources from value-added activities.

What about the predictability of elaborate gaming behaviours? Is it possible to foresee what shape the new gaming scenarios will take? Some strategies are quite well known and therefore relatively easy to anticipate. You are probably already familiar with some of them, and the examples throughout this book will have introduced you to many more. For instance, as we saw in the chapter on target setting, the so-called "ratchet effect" refers to the distortions created by introducing incrementally increasing targets, which may see people artificially lower the output this year to make next year's expected results more easily achievable. There are many other common effects associated with the introduction of measurement systems. However, because the structure, norms, routines and behaviours in every organization differ, there will be many gaming strategies that depend on context. If you introduce a performance measurement initiative in your own organization, predicting exactly which behaviours they will generate and especially how they will manifest themselves will be problematic. Really understanding your organization, its people, culture and routines becomes crucial here, because it is only after acquiring a deep knowledge of what is really happening on the ground will you be able to foresee the complex gaming scenarios that may develop.

LEARNING POINTS

Gaming and cheating are pervasive responses that can almost certainly be expected when an organization introduces a performance measurement initiative. As we have seen in this chapter, the consequences of such responses can be detrimental or even downright dangerous. However, these consequences are not inevitable.

In most organizations, managers have a broad set of levers through which they can bring about the intended effects and mitigate the detrimental ones. Dealing with gaming and cheating is no exception. Closing this chapter, we want to walk you through some of the options that are available to address these issues and prevent people's behaviour from sliding into gaming madness. These options range in scope from those that are more operational, and as such are aimed at addressing the simpler forms of gaming, to those that are concerned with the organization as a whole and deal with the deeper roots of gaming and cheating behaviours. Over the longer term, you have the opportunity to affect the factors that drive gaming, such as: reducing the intensity of performance measurement pressure; reviewing the type of performance targets; tightening the robustness of your data management systems; and changing your organizational climate.

Relieving the pressure

Firstly, you need to recognize that gaming and cheating are reactive behaviours. They arise in response to the pressures of various initiatives and most strongly in response to the pressure of performance measurement.

Therefore, you should aim to create a performance measurement system without undue negative performance measurement pressure. However, this takes time. One way to do so is not to rely on performance measurement as just a tool for evaluating performance and distributing rewards, but rather as an instrument for providing input into learning about the processes that generated a particular result. When performance measurement is seen as a learning practice rather than a system for assigning blame, the pressure to "make the numbers" is lifted, and the incentives to turn to gaming decrease dramatically. You can even take this a step further by using performance data to trigger and support the dialogue about the drivers of organizational performance. This is important at the corporate level, but even more so during individual performance reviews, shifting the focus from past results to future achievements.[30]

Setting the right kind of target

Besides the intensity of the pressure itself, the type of performance targets that are set for the individuals also influences the likelihood of gaming and cheating. We have discussed situations where people are more likely to turn to cheating when a uniform performance target is externally set for everybody and individual performance is compared to that of other people. In contrast, when targets are based on individual competence and are therefore personally meaningful to people, cheating dissipates. It is helpful, therefore, to have a target-setting process that reflects this. Working with colleagues, you would be better off introducing targets that are developmental and that increase employees' mastery of the tasks they are entrusted with, rather than impose an abstract performance standard that is supposed to work for everyone. This could be supported by other organizational practices, such as training, development and performance appraisals. Again, as it is with the case of performance measurement pressure, this approach to target setting emphasizes process over results and actual performance over numbers.

Foreseeing the future

As we have discussed, gaming and cheating behaviours differ in their scope and predictability. The scope of such behaviours ranges from minor interferences with performance data to elaborate strategies that involve multiple people and new behavioural patterns. Being able to foresee the extent of such behaviours is difficult.

Minor instances of data manipulation will not only be easier to foresee, for example, in which department it is likely to occur and what kind of data would be involved, but will also be easier to prevent than sophisticated gaming strategies that may spring up in response to a new performance measurement initiative. Management involvement before, during and after the introduction of such initiatives is therefore critical for gauging in advance both the scope and the kind of gaming that may appear. Talking to people helps to foresee what shape gaming is likely to take. Checking the impact of the newly introduced performance measurement initiative on the actual behaviours is absolutely crucial, as numbers can be particularly deceitful.

Improving data management systems

One of the quickest, but also perhaps the most short-lived and relatively expensive, ways of dealing with gaming is to improve the strength and robustness of your management control systems. In other words, if gaming occurs because things are allowed to slip through your fingers, the existing management control systems should be improved so that such slips are minimized. This is most relevant when dealing with performance data. As we saw earlier in this chapter, many gaming behaviours revolve around data: manipulation, misrepresentation and fabrication. In order to address these problems, you should look to improve data management practices, particularly in terms of timeliness, accuracy and trustworthiness.

One way to improve data quality is to introduce an end-to-end data management system that reflects the specific needs of your organization. So, for instance, if excessive data is a problem, such a system should focus on clarifying the purpose for data collection; and, if multiple data entry is required, the system should spell out the rules for doing so. Another way, of course, is to increase the strength of your management control over all data-related activities and discipline any offenders. Christopher Hood, a professor at Oxford University, has identified several ways the gaming of data can be dealt with[27]:

1. create tighter rules and data definitions and improve the IT system accordingly;
2. use multiple targets and performance indicators;
3. carry out unscheduled audits;
4. introduce severe punishment for offenders;
5. subcontract performance data collection to a third party.

Tighter data management is no doubt effective; however, it can often lead to yet another round of gaming. In other words, performance measurement drives gaming behaviours; those are dealt with through tighter measures and control, which can then lead to more sophisticated gaming...and, before you know it, you are in a downward spiral of cat-and-mouse, and the culture of gaming becomes pervasive. This is why tighter data management and management control are good for the short term, but for the longer term you may need to consider alternative approaches.

Changing the culture

Treating performance measures as instruments for learning and setting the right targets for individuals and teams are useful ways in which you can discourage gaming and cheating; although be aware that there may still be unintended consequences that your managers will need to deal with. Ideally, you want your employees to behave honestly and care about common goals; you also want them to flag up areas that can potentially be gamed; and, we are sure, you want them to improve their own performance and to help improve the performance of their colleagues. At the same time, what you don't want is for them to be thinking about how to game the system; or for your managers to be actively dealing with the consequences of such behaviour. Achieving all of this and thus minimizing gaming in the long term requires great organizational maturity. Such maturity requires mutual trust, goodwill, a culture of performance management as opposed to one of performance measurement and a general climate of collaboration rather than competition.

Trust is important because it makes possible those conversations about performance and performance management that we mentioned. Such conversations remove the pressure of performance measurement that drives gaming, but it only works if your people can trust that meaningful conversations are possible and that their input will not be used against them.

When you are thinking about the longer term, targets and data definitions that allow some degree of uncertainty are better and more valuable than tight guidelines and strict management control. This is because uncertainty and complexity can fuel the debates that help uncover the main drivers of performance. Any debate, however, should be approached from the premise that either side can be in the wrong. Therefore, goodwill is required both on the part of the managers and on the part of the employees. Goodwill, like trust, is what will allow the most valuable conversations about performance and performance management to flourish in your organization.

The way in which performance management becomes embedded in your organization's practices and routines will also be a key determinant of gaming. Looking at the use of performance information at different organizational levels, our own research shows that sometimes perverse behaviours are created by employees believing that performance management is just a numbers game with a fixation on performance targets.[31] In addition, because performance measurement systems are often regarded as monitoring mechanisms, this invariably leads to defensive responses and to the behaviours we have described in this chapter. Our study shows that this is not only dysfunctional, but it perpetuates a culture of performance *measurement*. Be aware that such a culture is much more likely to drive people to gaming and cheating because it is assumed that the making of the numbers is a key priority.

A completely different set of behaviours is instead related to a culture of performance *management* in which everyone has an understanding of the roles and functions of performance measurement in the organization as well as their dangers and limitations. Fostering a culture of performance management should be a key objective of your managers as you strive to create a long-term gaming-free environment.

Many organizations that have experienced the damaging consequences of gaming often find themselves returning to less quantitative but more holistic and longer-term oriented ways of managing performance. For instance, after all of the incidents with distorting crime figures in the UK police force, the new head of the Police Superintendents' Association of England and Wales explicitly proposed a step back from the obsession with numerical targets and "a return to common-sense policing, which focuses on doing the right thing for victims and the public".[32] Similarly, some American hospitals have successfully introduced performance management schemes that focus on the organizational culture and appeal to professional norms and pride rather than on specific performance targets.[33]

To conclude, as we saw earlier, a general climate of competitiveness is far more likely to generate gaming behaviours than a climate that encourages collaboration. Granted, some environments are inherently more competitive than others; however, wherever possible, if you want to limit the instances of gaming and cheating you should encourage collaboration and development rather than secrecy and competition. At the very least, the relative value and the inherent dangers of competitive organizational climates should be understood and made explicit.

AND FINALLY...

The thing to remember about gaming is that no amount of counter-gaming tactics can eradicate it if the general climate and atmosphere encourage it in the first place. The opening paragraphs of this chapter recounted the story of a pharmaceuticals company where a system of fines for arriving late in the morning provoked a major gaming response. When the employees' "solution" was finally discovered, the managing director took it in good spirit and abolished the fines, emphasizing, however, that no such behaviour would be tolerated in the future. However, just a few months later, a new scenario was discovered, this time in the purchasing department.

The purchasing managers who had built good relationships with the suppliers were routinely offered large discounts (sometimes up to 15%), either for the quantity they ordered or simply for being a loyal and trust-worthy customer. The managers, however, would refuse to take the discount in one go, asking the suppliers instead to break the 15% into a series of smaller discounts distributed over a longer period of time, say 2–3% per month over six months. What they would then do is show up at monthly management meetings reporting that they were "working flat out" on gaining supplier concessions and showing their success by regularly demonstrating their ability to gain yet another discount.

Hoping for A Whilst Rewarding B[1]

The English Premier League is one of the most prestigious soccer leagues in the world. Top players earn a vast amount of money in comparison to the man on the street. As with sportsmen and women in the majority of professional sports, fortune follows fame through the payment of higher salaries and the enhanced opportunity to endorse prestige products. The star of fame of an English Premier League footballer rises because of their individual prowess on the soccer pitch. Not only is there a league table of teams but there is also a league table for the top scorer in the season, and each team will also have their own internal table of the top scorers.

At the end of the 2009/10 season, Chelsea FC had to win their last match to secure the title. Didier Drogba, their top scorer, was on track to secure the accolade of highest scorer in the league. After taking a 1–0 lead, Chelsea were awarded a penalty kick. There then ensued a public altercation between Drogba and Frank Lampard, the regular penalty taker, over who was to take the kick. The situation was critical: a miss, and the pressure was back on Chelsea to win; a goal, and the championship was almost theirs. Drogba, with a visible display of anger, was forced to concede the kick to Lampard. It was reported that the manager, Carlo Ancelotti, had to calm Drogba down at half time. Fortunately for all concerned, Chelsea eventually won 8–0 and Drogba, who scored three goals in that match, received the Premier League's "Golden Boot".

Of course, scoring goals is a priority for any soccer team, but keeping the opposition from scoring is also of importance. Soccer is a team sport, where players can really only be acclaimed champions if they work together. So why then, when strong teamwork is known to lead to high achievement, do the league, the media and the sponsors place such emphasis on individual performance? Why do they *hope* for great teamwork but still *reward* individual prowess?

Hoping for teamwork, but rewarding individual effort, is just one example of introducing a mechanism to promote a certain behaviour, but ending up with a totally different outcome. Other similar and, alas, very common measurement pitfalls include hoping for long-term growth whilst rewarding short-term gains; hoping for defined outcomes whilst rewarding effort; and hoping for budgetary restraint whilst rewarding budgetary overspend.

This chapter will demonstrate that, although managers set out to reward people with all the right intentions, individuals will rationally focus on the elements that are rewarded, often without any reference to the initial goals set. For example, a good friend of one of the authors proudly boasted about her position in the health and fitness league table that had been initiated in her company, one of the UK's largest audit companies. In order to encourage their employees to work on their everyday fitness, every member of staff had been issued with a pedometer. A personal target was set across the company and a league table of results was maintained. For the competitive members of the organization, the friend included, there was the added challenge of considering how one travelled to the workplace, whether one walked to and from the train station, up and down the escalators, and around the office to meet colleagues. On the surface, this looked like a sound and well-intentioned programme. However, we are sure the instigators of this programme, who had hoped for a healthier workforce, did not realize that they would be rewarding higher levels of smoking. For the friend had quickly worked out that if she took more frequent cigarette breaks, which involved going up and down three flights of stairs, she could increase her pedometer mileage quite easily!

In Mike's opening story we saw how introducing elements of a measurement system, such as indicators, targets and rewards, with the specific aim of achieving something specific in fact led to something completely different. Mike had mandated the introduction of individual performance targets and regular performance reviews in order to enhance the overall productivity of the R&D department. However, the hoped-for enhanced unit performance through individual recognition had resulted in the R&D staff's disaffection and demotivation.

Although the next chapter will focus more specifically on reward and recognition schemes and their effects on behaviour, in this chapter we will also discuss some of the more common examples of how the misapplication of rewards can lead to unanticipated outcomes. One such example is that of the wiring contractors who were paid by the metre of wire laid. The hoped-for outcome was that they would lay the wire quickly and efficiently whereas in reality the contractors were rewarded for the quantity of wire that was laid. Needless to say, the electrical installers ran the wire, from the switch to the socket, up and down the wall cavity as many times as possible. So, rather than laying the 3m of cable needed, they actually laid 30m and claimed their reward.

Amusing though these anecdotes are, the serious side of why these phenomena exist is important, and it is essential to understand how to align measures, targets and rewards with the hoped-for outcomes, rather than introducing a measurement system loosely related to our goals and then being surprised when it takes us in a completely different direction.

COMMON MANAGEMENT REWARD FOLLIES

Hoping for teamwork whilst rewarding individual effort

Hoping for teamwork but rewarding individual effort is a principal example of management reward madness. However, please don't just think that this only applies to soccer teams; many organizations also have poorly designed systems, which engender behaviours that are by no means the fault of the individual employee.

Recently, on deciding to purchase a second-hand, nearly new, Mercedes-Benz, one of the authors, like any sensible purchaser, carried out research into what was available in the various dealerships. On the Internet it was possible to find an approved Mercedes-Benz network that had various dealerships around the country. Identifying a number of potential cars on the site, the author then proceeded to call the dealers to enquire about price and the possibility of a discount. Given that there were similar models at three of the different sites, the salesmen that the author spoke with all negotiated hard, each one of them keen to secure the sale. Eventually, after making the decision and physically visiting the preferred site to purchase the car, it became clear that all of the sites were in fact branches of the same company. In other words, the salesmen were undercutting each other, and the business was the only loser. Naturally, the author was curious as to the reasoning behind this behaviour. On questioning the Senior Sales Manager, it emerged that each salesman was rewarded on their individual sales, not on the hoped-for organizational profit.

Whilst examples thus far have focused on individuals, madness can also occur at the business unit level. A UK-wide distributor of heating and plumbing products based its business model on a branch network that primarily supplied products to local tradesmen. All branch managers prided themselves on the relationship they had with their customers, and wanted to keep their tradesmen satisfied so that they remained loyal to their branch. Each branch manager was rewarded on revenue in the hope that they would sell as much product as possible. Again, on paper this sounds like a sensible reward strategy. However, what typically happened was that a plumber – let's call him John – from the north of England, would be contracted to work on a job in central London. In carrying out the work, John would invariably find himself in need of plumbing supplies and he would telephone the nearest branch of his favourite supplier and obtain a quote. Then, John, being the loyal customer that he was, would also telephone his usual supplier branch, 200 miles away, to see if they could better the price on his order. The branch manager, being aware of his company's reward policy, would endeavour to undercut the price and then focus his effort in fulfilling the order. Of course, the branch manager would not want to pass the order on to his colleagues in London, as that would mean losing his revenue and missing his rewarded target. So, the branch manager would ensure that the order was filled, placed on the ubiquitous white van and driven overnight to London, so that John received his order the next working day. Needless to say, from a company point of view this was disastrous, as this process was often being repeated throughout the various branches. Not only was the company losing revenue due to one branch undercutting another, but the cost of fulfilling the order was far higher than if the nearest branch had supplied the order.

The question therefore is: why does this happen? Invariably, the reward systems at both Mercedes-Benz and the plumbing distributor were designed to engender good behaviours to increase revenues. Senior teams believed their reward systems would work, and each of the branches and dealerships took them on board. There was no maliciousness in gaming the system; all of the sales and branch managers believed they were doing what the company was hoping for. However, if you create a reward system that incentivizes the individual, it is very unlikely that this will promote team efforts.

In these examples, the organizations needed team incentives rather than individual incentives. Of course, in the presence of team incentives some people can freeload, taking the reward whilst relying on the effort of the other team members, but at least the company would not be losing profitable sales.

Hoping for the long term whilst rewarding short-term gain

There is a real tension in wanting to secure the long-term aims of an organization yet having to incentivize and set targets for the short term. Achieving this delicate balance is a real challenge for the shareholders of a company who hope for a steady return on their investment over the long term, whilst at the same time need to reward their executive teams with short-term share option plans – sometimes as short term as three years. Using such rewards, the incentive for the executive team is to grow the share price as quickly as possible over a three-year period, cash in the options and move onto the next challenge. The average tenure of a Fortune 500 CEO is 4.6 years[2] and, as this is an average, it indicates that many of them leave as soon as their share options mature.

This tension can endure at all levels of an organization, and can also materialize when benefits are taken out, as the following example illustrates. In a dot-com company, renowned for its creativity in non-contractual employee benefits, one of the perks of the job was that bread, butter and accompanying toppings were supplied free of charge. This meant that the techies could make themselves copious rounds of tea and toast throughout the day. Given that many of the staff were newly out of university, the free toast was of greater appeal to some than the company's generous pension contributions! As the year-end approached, and as this was a publicly quoted company, the finance director asked budget holders to identify where unnecessary expenditure could be cut. The facilities manager, newly promoted into the role and keen to make an impression, decided that cutting the free toast would be an easy and quick win. Well, the uproar that ensued nearly brought the company to a standstill. As the engineers explained, many of them came to work early, or stayed late to finish tasks, because they knew that breakfast or a late night snack would be available. They voiced their concern that if the toast was not reinstated then they would only work their contracted hours. The long-term benefits of a motivated and dedicated workforce, which the finance director knew would drive future profitability, were dangerously being undermined by his short-term cost-cutting exercise.

The tension between securing future revenues versus realizing immediate cost savings is a classic case of hoping for the long term but rewarding the short term. Another similar example to The Great Toast Scare is that of the organization that banned all landline phone calls before midday because the cost of calls was lower in the afternoon. The result was that sales effort was halved and long-term performance damaged, because the sales team were unable to contact their prospective clients for the best part of the working day.

Long term and short term are, of course, relative to the context and are at times cultural. For example, when in 1972 US President Richard Nixon asked China's Premier Zhou Enlai for his appraisal of the 1789 French Revolution, Zhou's reply was: "It is too early to say."

Although governments and public sector agencies should ideally take a long-term view, they are not immune to the dangers of being rewarded for short-term initiatives. Elected politicians are susceptible to focusing on short-term programmes that will show instant progress and hopefully get them re-elected. Public sector organizations often set short-term targets to improve current performance, but instead end up contradicting their longer-term aspirations. For example, where a police force has short-term targets for "crimes resulting in prosecution" this may be at the expense of investment into long-term crime detection and prevention programmes[3]; and teaching children to pass a test is not good for the long-term need for adaptable thinkers.

Hoping for truth whilst rewarding lies

Many of the stories told in the chapter on targets are fantastic examples of how individuals or teams will game a system in order to receive a reward. For example, do you remember the story about the purchasing managers in a small pharmaceuticals company in Russia who would receive large shipments of medical products from India that they had not ordered? The Indian company was hoping to sell more products to an ever-expanding market in Russia, but was actually rewarding the amount of shipments, not the amount of revenue received. Stories on the behaviours that accompany targets described a rather disturbing aspect of human nature. Surely, you may think that you would never display such behaviours, but, unfortunately, if you have ever been involved in a budgeting process, you might have inadvertently found yourself doing exactly that.

The budgeting process is one that engenders two types of dysfunctional behaviours. Firstly, the actual budgeting process itself is often a recognized corporate farce, where the participants are induced into playing along. In order to secure a favourable budget for the team, the initial budget is set artificially high, so that it can be reduced in a long and protracted cycle of budget negotiations. If the executives hope to manage the company through financial control, then they must be given accurate forecasts of potential spend. However, because individual managers are always subjected to hard negotiation, they are essentially rewarded for lying. Secondly, once the budget is set, a manager is then more often than not incentivized to deliver the performance against that budget. The organization rewards those that meet the target and punishes those that don't. However, it may be that those managers who meet their targets are gaming the system, whereas those who miss their targets may be doing the right things.

In recent years, one of the authors experienced the sales persons' gaming mentality whilst working in a recruiting agency environment. In this business, recruitment consultants were paid a commission for placing people in client organizations. If they placed under five people, they were paid a 5% commission of the billable value; if they placed between five and ten people they were paid a commission of 7.5%; and anything over ten was paid at 10%. The hope was that the consultants would place higher numbers of people in order to receive greater monetary reward. However, what actually happened was that, if the consultant had only placed three people this month and had one more person waiting to be offered a job, and it was towards the end of the month, she would persuade the client to defer the offer for a couple of days, with a variety of excuses. In so doing, the person awaiting the job would count towards the next month's total where the consultant was more likely to reach the higher threshold more quickly. Likewise, if the consultant had already reached the reward of 7.5% commission, she would get the offer to the candidate immediately, so that they could cash in on the placements at the higher level.

This perverse behaviour does not only manifest itself in sales departments and in the presence of company targets; it often occurs in customer reward point systems. For example, for some time one of the authors has been playing with the reward scheme developed by a well-known hotel chain where you are rewarded with different levels of membership. This system is so flawed that we really don't believe the company thought it through before implementing it. According to the scheme, you need to stay ten nights a year to qualify for silver level, 50 nights for gold and 75 nights for platinum. The incentive to reach the higher reward levels is that you then receive greater service, free upgrades, free breakfasts and even more reward points, which can then be redeemed against further hotel stays. The initial reward system was quite simple: the company hoped that clients would stay more and therefore offered rewards with differing levels of service and freebies. However, in 2009 the company realized that customers were unhappy if they had stayed for 45 nights throughout the year and then the annual clock clicked over and was reset back to zero. Where was the incentive for the customer to build up to nearly 50 nights, after spending $10,000? So, the hotelier, in its wisdom, decided that if you had not reached the next level, you could roll over the nights to the next year. Again, this sounds sensible, on paper. However, this policy has a major flaw. For example, for a customer who may have reached 49 nights by 30th December, this means one more stay to reach gold level. One option therefore is to stay at the hotel for New Year's Eve and click up to the 50 nights. However, in this case, on 1st January all 50 nights would be removed, the clock would be reset and you would need to stay 75 nights the following year to reach platinum level. The other option is to play the numbers and therefore not stay on New Year's Eve, but carry forward the 49 nights to the following year. Thus, now only 26 more days would be needed to reach platinum status. This scheme presents a clear incentive for customers to delay their stay if, towards the end of the year, they are reaching the threshold of the next level of reward.

Delaying spend on a hotel room or pushing a placement into the next month to earn a favourable bonus, although costly to the organization, may not appear excessively worrying – surely, these are just harmless ploys. However, the bigger the stakes, the more extreme the madness becomes, and the more likely we are to enter the territory of gaming and cheating. Indeed, some forms of cheating can be far more serious and can have a premeditated aspect to playing the game. As the examples of Informix and Enron in the chapter on target setting demonstrated, such actions can have more detrimental effects on an organization and, taken to extremes, can be regarded as fraud. When it happens at an individual level, it is seen as a clever bit of manoeuvring to get an extra bonus; when it happens at the business unit level, it is seen as the standard game that is played to get a reasonable budget; but when it happens at the organizational level and unaware shareholders are being defrauded, this can actually become a criminal offence. Therefore, when you are hoping for truthful figures to enable performance planning or for investment decisions, do not set rewards that will lead to inadvertent gaming or, in extreme cases, outright cheating.

Hoping for contribution whilst rewarding outcomes

When most graduates reminisce about their student days, they inevitably begin by fondly recalling the fun and social side of the experience, and then, more often than not, the quality of the teaching they received or the knowledge they gained at the knee of a renowned professor. In large undergraduate universities teaching is paramount, as this is the cash cow of the profession, and student satisfaction scores play an important role in prospective students' decisions over where to apply. Therefore, you would expect that, if university leaders hope for excellence in teaching quality for their high paying consumers, then they would reward their academics for this. Reality is actually quite different: university careers are made or lost on the number of high ranking publications that academics achieve and teaching is virtually never considered. A professor gains kudos through the research that is undertaken, and a measure of the quality of that research is the level of peer-reviewed journals that the research is published in. Therefore, although the higher governing bodies hope for teaching contribution and quality, academics are rewarded for high publication rates in top quality journals.

It could be argued, in a similar vein, that society hopes that those very students who are being taught by those disincentivized academics are gaining knowledge and learning new ways of thinking so as to improve their society in the future. However, many students learn quickly that their priority is to pass exams, rather than to learn challenging subjects, and therefore spend most of their time working out how to pass tests. In the end, society hopes that students will expand their minds and be better citizens, yet rewards them for achieving good grades.

An interesting commercial example has arisen recently with the continued popularity of low cost airlines. As the base cost of a ticket is competitively used to attract passengers, the low cost industry has had to find other ways of raising revenues. Although Ryanair has been reported to be considering charging people for using the on-board toilets,[i] most of the carriers have restricted their practices to only charging for luggage that needs to be placed in the hold. However, canny travellers now pack as much as possible into their permitted hand luggage, so as to save on this additional charge. A money saving expert has even designed a specialist travel jacket with pockets for additional items such as laptops.[ii] So, where the airlines were hoping for additional revenue contribution, they have been rewarded with ingenious packing solutions. Interestingly, this practice has now gone full circle, as the airlines now no longer have enough cabin space for all of the hand baggage and therefore have to offer passengers free carriage in the hold for their well-packed luggage.

Many of the stories on target setting in Chapter 6, and gaming in Chapter 7, recognized the issue of rewarding outcomes rather than attaining the hoped-for contribution. As we saw in the Mid Staffordshire hospital example, the hospital board of governors was hoping that all of their A&E patients would be seen within four hours, but actually only rewarded the focus on easy-to-treat patients rather than all patients.

Hoping for budget control whilst rewarding overspend

It was approaching year-end in the busy maternity ward on floor C and in the geriatric ward on the ground floor at one of our local hospitals. Both departments had had a good year with over 1,000 babies safely delivered and over 500 hips replaced. Achieving each of these health-related targets had been at some expense; however, the maternity ward had yet to spend a large proportion of its budget on its much-needed premature baby incubators. The geriatric ward, however, had already overspent its budget on preventive initiatives aimed at reducing the incidents of broken hips, and therefore decreasing future expenditure. Given that the medical supply company was about to introduce new incubators at a much higher price, the maternity department was considering delaying its purchase for a couple of months in order to buy old stock at reduced prices.

---

[i] Gordon, S. (2010) Ryanair confirms it WILL bring in charges for on-board toilets. *Mail Online*, 6 Apr., online at: http://www.dailymail.co.uk/travel/article-1263905/ Ryanair-toilet-charges-phased-in.html.
[ii] Lewis, M. (2010) 'The jacket' to beat budget airline fees, *MoneySavingExpert. com*, 7 Jul, online at: http://www.moneysavingexpert.com/news/travel/2010/07/ where-to-get-the-jacket-to-beat-budget-airline-fees.

In setting the budgets, the hospital administrators had hoped that each department would operate within its financial boundaries. Given this hope, which of the two departments would be rewarded for their prudency in achieving their financial and clinical outcomes? Logic would say that it should be the maternity ward, and it should be rewarded with the money to buy the incubators next year, whereas the future savings of the geriatric ward should be recognized and its budget reviewed downwards for the coming year. However, in many organizations the philosophy is "use it or lose it", and, in this case, this is exactly what happened. The maternity ward decided that, as it would not receive the money the following year, it would be better off buying the incubators at the current price and making sure it used up the entire budget. The geriatric ward, instead, had spent today to make savings for tomorrow, but was rewarded with a slightly higher budget, as it was deemed that there was an obvious need for it.

This situation is not uncommon in private sector companies either. Once a budget has been hard won, it becomes imperative to spend it, so that it is not lost! Training and development budgets are a classic example of this phenomenon, and we are often reminded of this in our work in academia and consultancy; very often a potential company or graduate student will enquire as to whether they can pay for the whole course up front, as the training money is in this year's budget and may not be available next year.

In May 2013, NBC's Channel 4 I-Team reported that the Tennessee Department of Labor and Workforce Development had been rewarded with a payment of $1.3 million despite an audit that showed that they had wasted $73 million on unemployment benefits, paying out to dead people and prisoners.[4] At around the same time, nearly 150 employees attended a residential training conference at a four-star hotel, enjoying all the amenities on offer, and spending $86,000 of the government's reward. Why did the department receive this reward if their performance was so poor? The problem was that in this case the budget had been split into different streams of money, and, although the wasted amounts were for the overpayment of unemployment insurance, the reward was for the department's performance in training jobseekers and helping them find long-term employment. In fact, the conference was held to consolidate best practices and therefore cut future wastage. Splitting up the budget into different lines can give the illusion of better financial control, but any reward should look at the current status and overall performance of the organization. Similarly, it is of little use saving money on your own household food bills only to blow your savings on an overseas holiday.

LEARNING POINTS

What can you take away from these stories? It is easy to see the consequences of measurement madness, but more difficult to ascertain what caused them or how to mitigate the risk of them occurring in your own organization.

Targets, rewards and measures

Over the last few decades, there has been an increasing focus on the use of simple, quantifiable measures and associated targets supposedly to motivate people towards the hoped-for outcome. The use of these systems has been lauded as the way to gain extra performance from employees, with a view that, given a monetary reward for achieving a stretch target, it will garner even greater effort. However, as we have seen in the various examples above and in the previous chapter, if we do not consider how people might – consciously or subconsciously – behave, we may well end up rewarding the wrong outcome.

Rewarding performance through the use of one easily quantifiable measure is one of the main pitfalls when you set a target expecting it to lead to a particular result. As we have recounted, attributing the reward to a single quantifiable target often leads to an inadvertent, or even a deliberate, change in behaviour. Therefore, our first piece of advice is that, if you must set a reward, you would be better off introducing a qualitative measure alongside the quantitative one. Also, although this may help, please be aware that the system may still not be perfect. The case of an outsourced technical support centre illustrates the point nicely. Having carried out an enormous amount of analysis, and run and rerun the figures, a large European telecommunication company decided, for cost efficiency purposes, to outsource the support of the box that controlled their home broadband and TV delivery. The business had worked out the number of support calls they received on average and had determined a cost per call. The support centre company was to be paid on the number of calls answered; this essentially meant that they were incentivized to deal with as many calls as possible. The world of call centres is littered with bad examples of performance measurement, such as improving the number of calls answered by simply picking up the telephone receiver and placing it straight down again. The telecom was aware of this, and so it placed a qualitative measure on the staff, which meant they had to engage with the customer and give the customer instructions on how to fix the problem. In spite of this, gaming ensued: when customers called with a problem, they were deliberately given the wrong advice, which meant that the customers had to telephone again to have their problem solved. Therefore, the telecoms company had effectively introduced a measurement system to reward good customer service, but had ended up promoting the opposite outcome.

Gaming has already featured heavily in the consequences of measurement; however, in this chapter we have also described a number of instances where the behaviour has not necessarily been premeditated – rather, it was mainly the system that drove the wrong behaviour. One of the key problems is that, as with measurement in general, it is easier to emphasize the visible behaviours than those that are harder to observe. For example, in 2001 the US administration introduced the "No Child Left Behind Act", which tied the distribution of federal funding to schools to the measurable standards of basic skills in reading, writing and arithmetic. The hope was to increase the emphasis on the teaching of basic educational skills. However, schools across the country then drastically cut the time and resources dedicated to non-assessed subjects and redirected them to the teaching of English and mathematics. Moreover, students who did not do well in English and mathematics classes were precluded from taking any other subjects and sent to remedial classes...in English and mathematics. Although not bad *per se*, the outcome of this initiative meant that children were no longer receiving a well-rounded education.

Therefore, rather than reward a hoped-for outcome on one or maybe a couple of simple countable numbers, you may wish to look at the use of more subjective, longer-term, qualitative measures. As we have previously discussed, quantitative measures are often used because they are easy to set and to understand, and the data are readily available. This could be a reason why the highest number of individual goals scored in the English Premier League is rewarded. However, even in sports, the use of qualitative measures is still relevant. Each year, sports writers and players vote for their favourite player of the year. This vote reflects subjective judgement, but it is not one that anyone can game; nominated players have to do exceptionally well all season to be rewarded. In a business environment it is often difficult for managers to evaluate how well an individual or a team has contributed to, or been detrimental to, the desired outcome. One way of achieving this is to bring in a degree of subjectivity into the performance evaluation, by canvassing different perspectives and facilitating dialogue, so as to ensure that the hoped-for result is the one that is really rewarded.

Reward people later

An issue with long-term versus short-term thinking is that organizations normally pay the reward or bonus on completion of the short-term objective. Although the short term may be a month for recruitment consultants, or three years for CEOs, the bonus could be paid much later on, when the outcome of people's actions can be fully determined and to mitigate short-term focused dysfunctional behaviours. For example, the recruitment consultants could be paid their commission once a year or when they leave the company; and the senior executives of a company could be paid their options ten years after their maturity date (interestingly, this practice is becoming more common in various industries). Imagine the potential change in behaviour if a senior public servant was only paid a pension after their long-term contribution to society had been assessed; say 20 years after leaving office.

Avoid negative spillover

Setting new rewards in order to change behaviours and outcomes will often give people a licence to act in new, unexpected ways. A recent study looked at the effect of placing recycling bins next to the paper towels in public toilets.[5] The aim of such a move was to encourage users to recycle the paper rather than just throw the towels into the general waste bins. In order to encourage the "right" behaviour, signs, explaining the recycling programme, were also placed next to the paper towel dispensers. However, when the researchers measured the number of hand towels used before and after the new system, they discovered a large increase in the number of paper towels being used. The suggested explanation is that the toilets' users felt that they now had a licence to use more paper towels as they were now going to be recycled. Therefore, we should be careful that the message we are sending out doesn't legitimize a different, negative behaviour.

Systems thinking

A major learning point of this chapter should be that many organizations focus on hitting the target, but totally miss the point of the exercise. Like the Mercedes-Benz car salesmen who were willing to undercut their colleagues because they were unaware that the real target was overall company revenue, or the builders' merchants who would supply their tradesmen across the country because they didn't understand the value of the company network. Therefore, you need to check regularly whether the focus is on the overall objective, rather than just on the target.

One of the other problems in using multiple measures when they are not joined up within a system is that people do not understand what the priorities are or what the trade-offs should be if a clash occurs. As we saw in Chapter 6, for almost two decades the UK government has been determined to impose targets on all aspects of the health system in order to drive efficiencies and improve effectiveness. On one stormy night in early winter, an ambulance crew was called to an accident. They arrived quickly, meeting their target, administered the first line of medical care and transported the patient to the local hospital, again within the expected time span. On arriving at A&E, they were told by the administrative manager that A&E could not accept the patient, as they were incredibly busy and they were going to miss the four-hour waiting time target. However, the ambulance crew were adamant that they had to deliver the patient otherwise they would miss their delivery target and they would not be able to attend to other emergencies.[6] The very short-term solution would have been to leave the patient in the car park! Fortunately, this never happened, but you can understand how such madness can be caused by a misaligned system of measures. The implication here is that, when implementing a performance measurement system, it is imperative to consider the bigger picture and to relate measures and targets to the overall goals of the organization. In this example, the goals were patient care and saving lives, not arrival and waiting times.

AND FINALLY...

This final story emphasizes all the points made in this chapter. Remember to be careful about setting quantifiable and easily gamed targets; be careful about the behaviour that the measure will engender; and try to make sure that everyone understands the reasoning behind the measure.

In many countries across the world, governments have been concerned with the high rate of road deaths. Multiple studies show that the high speed of a vehicle is a key factor in such fatal accidents. Given that the police cannot patrol every inch of the highway, authorities in many of these countries have introduced the physical presence of speed cameras with the hope that drivers will drive more sensibly given their fear of being fined, losing their licence or, at worst, being sentenced to a prison term. However, very quickly the general driving public have adapted their behaviour by slowing down only for the camera and then reverting to their original speed; often with the aid of electronic devices that warn of the up and coming camera. As drivers no longer have to worry about mobile and unexpected police vehicles checking their speed, once they have passed the cameras the drivers are essentially rewarded by fewer chances of being caught or punished.

9

Failing Rewards and Rewarding Failure

Since the Most Excellent Order of the British Empire was established in 1917, many men and women have been created knights or dames by the British Crown for their services and work in government, the military, business and the arts. Being awarded a knighthood is a prestigious matter and a great honour, although no monetary reward is associated with the award. On the flipside is the more serious fate of being stripped of an honour: not only is this a grave affair, but it is also incredibly rare.

On 31st January 2012, Fred Goodwin, former CEO of the Royal Bank of Scotland (RBS), was stripped of the honour given to him in 2004 for services to banking, thus losing his title of "Sir". In the past, only those convicted of an actual criminal offence or those struck off professional bodies had suffered such ignominy. Mr Goodwin also joined an auspicious list of those honorary knights who had also been stripped of their title, such as Robert Mugabe, Nicolae Ceauşescu and Benito Mussolini. How could this happen? Was what Mr Fred Goodwin did so bad that he could be compared with such notorious figures?

Apparently, his services to banking had not been particularly valuable. Under his helm, between 2005 and April 2008, RBS raised a record-breaking £12 billion in cash just months after acquiring Dutch bank ABN Amro. Unfortunately, the aforementioned deal had left RBS unable to absorb the "credit crunch" losses, and the British taxpayer had to put in £45 billion to keep the bank afloat.[1] The chairman of the Financial Services Authority affirmed that the organization's approach was "seriously flawed",[2] and that RBS' capital position was too weak to proceed with the takeover of parts of ABN Amro.[i] Although this was one of the largest failures in the history of banking, certainly no one person alone could have created such a disastrous situation. However, Fred Goodwin was the primary decision-maker at RBS at the time,[3] and, rightly or wrongly, attracted all the attention *post factum*.

---

[i] Too bad this was stated after things had already gone wrong. However, as it sometimes happens in the otherwise grey history of management, punctuated by typically modest achievements and improvements, a miracle occurred in the very place where disasters had been provoked: during 2011 the "culture of banks changed" (RBS chairman Sir Philip Hampton) BBC news website, 20 December 2011, online at: http://www.bbc.co.uk/news/business-16135247.

Even though the decision about whether to strip Mr Goodwin of his honour was widely discussed in political circles and in the media, the real debate was not so much about *awards*, but, rather, about *rewards*. During his final year in charge Fred Goodwin was paid £4.2 million, which included a bonus of £2.86 million, he had a pension pot of £8.37 million and he owned £2.53 million worth of shares in RBS. These financial rewards were there to remunerate and incentivize his performance. The real question is: what effect did these rewards actually have?

The recent financial crisis has undeniably put rewards in the spotlight, and a growing number of commentators have become increasingly vocal in questioning the very idea of using financial incentives in organizations. Some have even described the whole question of recognition and rewards as "a minefield of ideology and misinformation".[4] In the story that opened this book, several of Mike's colleagues lamented the use of financial rewards; the old Chief Operating Officer had even referred to them as "bribes". The CEO of the IT subsidiary, instead, decided to scrap them, as they were perceived to be the cause of gaming and cheating.

As we will see in this chapter, one of the problems with financial incentives is that they are overused and often regarded as an answer to every problem; from senior management performance to poor customer service, from failing schools to low performing hospitals.[5] Although there is ample evidence to suggest that motivation and the desire to achieve are driven by many more factors than just a financial reward, the introduction of pay-for-performance schemes in both private and public organizations is at an all-time high. Why is this and how could it be?

This chapter is not a manifesto against financial rewards. Pay and financial rewards are certainly important for individuals, as they are not only a means to an end, but they are also associated with social status and perceptions of individual achievement. Also, they play an important role in attracting and retaining employees. What we wish to discuss here is whether the use of financial incentives in a measurement system can lead to *better performance* at the individual level and, therefore, at the organizational level. In other words, by using financial incentives are we getting any better at what we do?

In this chapter, we will review the use of financial incentives in a variety of contexts and show you how their use often amplifies both the positive and the negative consequences of performance measurement described in previous chapters. In particular, we will illustrate the important and sometimes counterintuitive links between measurement, rewards, motivation and behaviours. We will begin by reviewing, albeit briefly, some of the key arguments and evidence for and against the use of financial rewards with performance measures. We will then question some of the basic assumptions of the principal and agent model, which has been used repeatedly to support the introduction of extrinsic motivators, especially financial rewards. Finally, we will propose ways to introduce "good" rewards, which, when properly connected to a performance measurement system, can motivate individuals and lead to enhanced organizational performance.

TOP REWARDS FOR TOP PERFORMERS

In 1990, Michael Jensen, Professor of Business Administration at Harvard Business School, along with his colleague Kevin Murphy, wrote a seminal piece, which argued that in most publicly held companies the compensation of top executives was virtually independent of performance.[6] However, excessive pay was not deemed to be the issue. On the contrary, Jensen and Murphy claimed that the levels of CEO compensation were not high enough to attract the best performers.[6] Indeed, at the time, the authors' hope was that more aggressive pay-for-performance systems would become the norm so that poorer performing executives would more likely be dismissed for missing their targets, and less capable managers would in fact be offered lower compensation. In such a situation, there would be attractive financial incentives for the more able and more motivated executives to perform better than their peers. The belief was that, if executives were paid more to enhance organizational performance, they would find ever more "creative ways" to achieve their goals.[6] Thus, the gap between executive compensation and performance would close.

After nearly a quarter of a century later, on a positive note, we can say that Jensen and Murphy were right in two ways. Firstly, in 1990 pay and performance were indeed virtually disconnected; secondly, over the past two decades, the pay of executives has risen, probably to levels that were unimaginable back then. Looking at variations in executive pay, a report estimated that, in 2010 alone, this rose 50% at the UK's top firms, taking the average pay for a director of a FTSE 100 company to approximately £2.7 million.[7] This report also stated that: "Britain's economy may be struggling to return to pre-recession levels of output, but the same cannot be said of FTSE 100 directors' remuneration."[8] The gap between high and low pay in the UK had become such a contentious issue that, in November 2010, an independent body, the High Pay Commission, was set up to investigate the reasons for the gap. The Commission found that average annual bonuses, which were worth 48% of salary in 2002, were worth 90% in 2011. The Commission concluded that such high salaries of UK executives were actually "corrosive" for the economy.

However, what Jensen and Murphy got wrong was that, despite considerable use of pay-for-performance in conjunction with performance measurement systems, pay and performance are still pretty much independent. Also, except in the case of Fred Goodwin at RBS, dismissal for poor performance is still very rare. The High Pay Commission estimated that although the average bonus of a director of a FTSE 350 company had risen by 187% in the 2002–2011 period, there was no corresponding rise in share prices. This led the Commission chair, Deborah Hargreaves, to question the "myth" that big bonuses meant companies performed better.[9] This latter point is particularly relevant because a fundamental reason given for introducing financial incentives, and measurement systems more broadly, is to reward behaviours and actions that lead to improved business performance. In other words, objectives, targets, indicators and rewards are tools used to motivate employees, and provide direction and alignment towards the achievement of organizational goals. But do financial rewards really do that?

REWARDING FAILURE

The case of the American Insurance Group's Financial Products (AIG FP) is a striking example of rewards given to people who had clearly achieved disappointing results. The meltdown at AIG FP has been described as "what happens when short, bald managers of otherwise boring financial bureaucracies start seeing Brad Pitt in the mirror".[10] But what happened exactly? Well, the FP group created such liabilities in AIG's credit default swap portfolio that it brought the company down. Similar to the example of RBS in the UK, it became 80% government owned and required an injection of $170 billion of taxpayers' money. Subsequent to the government bailout, the company then announced a quarterly loss of over $60 billion.[11] Somewhat surprisingly, AIG decided to reward such a "performance" with over $165 million in bonus payments to the 400 units of the FP group. These bonuses were in addition to the not exactly meagre salaries: Joe Cassano, who had spent 20 years at AIG, and was the head of the Financial Products division until the very end, had received $280 million in cash and an additional $34 million in bonuses throughout his career. Even after he was forced to resign in March 2008, he was retained on the AIG payroll, earning a reportedly $1 million a month in consulting fees despite his role in "the probable downfall of Western civilization".[10] And note: all of this had happened after taxpayers had been forced to step in and rescue AIG. The CEO, Martin Sullivan, defended his decision to Congress saying that AIG wanted to "retain the 20-year knowledge that Mr. Cassano had."

The collapse of AIG is obviously an extreme case of rewarding failure; fortunately, financial rewards are often used in better ways. However, this and similar cases that happened in the late 2000s are particularly significant, as they were predicted by commentators. In 2005, Raghuram Rajan, the then Chief Economist of the International Monetary Fund, had spoken about huge financial incentives related to short-term profits and that imposed no penalties for subsequent losses. According to Rajan, such incentives could encourage bankers to take risks so high that their own firms, or even the entire financial system, could be brought to their knees.[12] Clearly, too few people listened, and we were left with disastrous situations in organizations that were "too big to fail". Could the situation at AIG and elsewhere have been prevented? We believe so, and we think that a sensible use of performance measurement and rewards could have helped; we shall return to this later in the chapter.

FAILING REWARDS

Pay-for-performance is not exclusively linked to financial services, nor is it restricted to senior management of private firms. Indeed, pay-for-performance schemes have been tried and tested in most industrial sectors and organizations, albeit with repeatedly unconvincing results. The fundamental assumption behind these schemes is quite appealing: the performance of individuals and teams is measurable; financial rewards motivate people and therefore align behaviours; and connecting measurement and rewards is pretty straightforward.

The attraction of such an appealing argument is also reflected in the attempts by several governments to adopt performance-related pay practices in different areas of the public sector, from central to local government, from police forces to healthcare. For example, as we write this book, many countries are looking at introducing or reviewing pay-for-performance schemes in schools. In the UK, debates over measurement and reward for teachers' performance have been going on for years, oscillating between great hope when performance indicators and incentives are introduced, and frustration when a decision is taken to scrap them. In May 2012, an influential cross-party group of MPs in Westminster recommended the introduction of a new pay-for-performance scheme in order to prevent the worst teachers from taking advantage of a "rigid and unfair" salary structure. Even though such an argument is difficult to oppose, as few would argue that good and bad performers should be paid the same, reactions were mostly adverse, with the general secretary of the main teachers' union stating that payment by results was a "total nonsense".[13] You might expect such a negative response by the unions to a centre-right government initiative, but you might also think that head teachers would be more in favour, since they would be the first to benefit from a scheme that aims at attracting, training and retaining the best teaching talent.[14] But, no: several head teachers of English schools argued that such a scheme would pit teachers against each other and would destroy any notion of teamwork.[15] In fact, the profession was worried that rewards would not only fail to boost performance, but might actually lead to worse results. Interestingly, a popular suggestion after this proposal was to introduce performance-related pay for Members of Parliament!

In a similar vein, in 2010, the Italian Ministry of Education launched an initiative to reward their "best teachers". Teachers' performance was to be measured as the degree of convergence between the opinions of students, parents and colleagues over the quality of every teacher's professional reputation. Therefore, a good teacher would be recognized as such by three different stakeholder groups. Whilst this scheme was certainly more sophisticated than the simple recording of students' test results, it was strongly opposed by the unions and was eventually cancelled on the grounds that it included monetary incentives for individual teachers. In 2012, it was reframed as a scheme to reward the best schools, which attracted much more interest and the willing participation of many more schools.[16]

Although pay-for-performance in education may seem pretty radical, it is not: in the USA, such schemes were already widely in place as far back as 1918. And what have we learned over almost a century later? According to management professors Jeff Pfeffer and Bob Sutton, very little: "evidence shows that merit-pay plans seldom last longer than five years and that merit pay consistently fails to improve student performance".[5] Why is this? Surely, if you pay teachers more for improving student grades, those teachers will do all they can to develop their pupils. However, such a premise is based on flawed logic and an unrealistic set of assumptions: firstly, it assumes that teacher motivation is a determinant, perhaps even *the* determinant, of student learning and achievement; secondly, that learning can be measured reliably and accurately by a test given once a year; thirdly, that teachers are motivated largely, or at least significantly, by financial incentives; and finally, that teaching is a solo activity and that has little interdependence with others in the school.[5]

According to Pfeffer and Sutton, these assumptions are unrealistic and undermine the credibility and potential success of any pay-for-performance scheme in education, as the UK and Italian governments discovered. The examples from these two countries are also interesting because they shed light on another very important matter for rewarding performance – the difference between individual and team-based incentives; something that we will examine towards the end of this chapter.

MEASUREMENT, REWARDS AND MOTIVATION

Given the numerous examples of the perverse effects of rewards, why are they such an integral part of many performance measurement systems, and why do we believe they work in the first place? Just as there are two sides to every coin, so there are two sides to every business. In the context of performance measurement and rewards, we talk about two parties: the principal and the agent. The role of the principal, for example the business owner, is to supply capital, bear the risk and delegate work to the "hired hands" – his or her agents. The agent's role is to work for the principal, which involves effort as well as decision-making responsibilities. One potential issue that arises in such an arrangement is that the world looks quite different depending on where you sit, so the principal and the agent may want very different things. The classic approach to solving this issue is based on the belief that financial rewards help align the interests of the two parties. In a listed company, for example, the principal can be thought of as a shareholder, and the agent as the CEO and/or the top executive team. In this case, a pay-for-performance package granted to the CEO is one of the means for the shareholders to control and direct the CEO's efforts, so that he or she will aim to achieve results that are in the shareholders' interest.

Such reasoning is not unfounded, as evidence from research and practice shows that pay and the opportunity to receive financial rewards are key factors for recruiting people. For example, by offering strong individual financial incentives, an organization can signal its willingness to attract competitive individuals more than if it stated that rewards and promotions were purely based on seniority.[5] Secondly, several studies have shown that employees are likely to respond more effectively to financial incentives than to any other motivational intervention. Thirdly, especially in some national cultures, pay is often used as a yardstick for social status.[17]

Whilst the principal–agent relationship is regarded as fundamental for the good functioning of an organization, and financial incentives can be used to align the goals of both parties, there are two significant issues to take into account. The first is one is the so-called "moral hazard", where problems can arise due to the conflicting interests of both parties and to the fact that it is difficult or expensive for the principals to verify the agents' actions. In many situations, the principal cannot directly observe whether the agent is behaving appropriately. The agents can then use this to pursue their own objectives that may be very different from the objectives of their employers. For example, in the absence of direct control from the shareholders, senior management may be tempted to divert profits towards nice perks and benefits: corporate jets, expensive offices, generous severance packages and the like.

The second problem is one of "adverse selection", which arises because of the different levels of information the principal and the agent have regarding, for example, the agent's skills or private interests. Think of it this way: when people buy home insurance, they probably have a much better idea about the state of their houses than the insurance providers do. Because of this disparity in the level of information, insurance providers run the risk of issuing cheap insurance premiums to those who own decrepit houses and who can therefore become a huge liability in the future. Likewise, senior managers usually have a better estimate of their own abilities than their boards do. However, because the managers are not likely to share this information, the board always risks appointing a less-than-competent senior management team.

Both the moral hazard and the adverse selection problems lead to a loss in efficiency and a reduction in organizational value. Both can be addressed through performance measurement and management, but in two different ways: the first is to keep collecting information about the agents' actions by investing in information and performance measurement systems; the second is to design a compensation contract that links the outcome of the agents' actions to the compensation they receive; for example, a pay-for-performance contract. In theory, if the principal's information system accurately reports the agent's actions, and if the compensation contract motivates the agent to focus on achieving the principal's goals, then any manipulation would be detected, the interests would be aligned and the adverse selection and moral hazard would be eliminated. This means that the principal's expected goals are more likely to be achieved. In other words, (at least in theory) managers will be more motivated to pursue the organization's objectives. You can easily see how the principal–agent relationship is the main theoretical argument used to support the introduction of pay-for-performance schemes.

While these arguments are all relevant, our question is not simply one of whether pay matters; rather, it is more one of whether pay and, in particular, pay-for-performance really do drive individual and organizational performance. It is when trying to answer this question that some of the assumptions made by proponents of the principal–agent model start to crack and buckle. Proponents of financial rewards postulate that agents will work harder to achieve objectives when their pay is contingent on their performance.[17] A study that supports such a claim is a field experiment of tree planters in British Columbia, Canada. This research examined the incentive effects of monetary compensation schemes on individual performance, and found that workers' productivity increased by 20% when they were moved from fixed wages to piece rates.[18] However, how representative is the job of tree planters when we consider the intricacies of most organizational structures; the difficulty in separating individuals' contributions; and the challenges in observing, let alone quantifying, their outputs?

True, those who argue in favour of financial rewards often advocate their use in contexts in which "individual contributions are separable and where performance can be measured objectively".[19] A good example, therefore, would be the American Pulpwood Association we mentioned in the chapter on target setting, where individual targets and rewards led to significant increases in the productivity of loggers. However, once again, one wonders how significant are the contexts and job characteristics of tree loggers. If we look at more typical organizational settings, sales functions are arguably the closest environments where "separable individual contributions" and "objective measures of performance" can be found. The assumption is that sales performance can be traced to a particular sales executive's effort and can be objectively measured, and that pay-for-performance will drive each person to push harder. However, as we discussed in the previous chapter, not all sales achievements are necessarily down to hard work, and in the case of the Mercedes-Benz dealerships, individual targets and rewards led to poorer company performance.

The underlying principles of agency theory may work in a number of cases, but, in this day and age, organizations and work are increasingly complex and, more often than not, output is dependent on collaboration, as opposed to the simple sum of individual efforts. Furthermore, as you will have learnt through reading this book, one should always be sceptical when the words "performance measurement" and "objectively" are used in the same sentence. As we discussed earlier, in practice, pay, and particularly variable pay, are very difficult to connect to performance.

WHEN FINANCIAL REWARDS BACKFIRE

Whilst a number of studies have confirmed the relevance of pay for recruiting people and directing attention, they are often silent in relation to what interests us most in this chapter: whether and how financial rewards in a measurement system affect individual and organizational performance. In contrast, there is a growing body of evidence on the negative effects of pay-for-performance. Firstly, our story about Fred Goodwin may have made you think that flawed compensation arrangements have been confined to a number of "bad apples". However, please don't be fooled, such examples have been, and still are, widespread, persistent and systemic.[20] Also, the missing link between measurement and pay and performance is not necessarily an unfortunate accident; it is often intentional: the use of pensions, golden parachute payments and high bonuses are mechanisms used to effectively increase base pay. The use of complex reward packages weakens, rather than strengthens, the link between performance, measurement and rewards.

Secondly, pay-for-performance, especially at the executive level, may be regarded as financially negligible. Unfortunately, financial implications are significant, as a study conducted in the mid-2000s was able to demonstrate.[20] It was shown that for the companies studied, the cost of compensating their top five executives was 9.8% of the earnings for their firms, and, therefore, if that compensation were reduced, or even cut, shareholders would receive a much greater return. However, as it has been clearly demonstrated by recent failures in curbing executive pay and bonuses in financial services, reducing the amount of compensation or making changes to a reward scheme is difficult to achieve.

Thirdly, even though theoretically managers should have little influence over pay- after all, financial rewards should be a mechanism to align the managers' interests to those of the owners- in reality this is rarely so. Managers have been found to hold a "smoking gun" when it comes to pay. They do not necessarily hold the business to ransom, but they use their power to obscure the link to their performance and negotiate generous benefits in case of their early departure.[20] This is yet more evidence that the link between financial rewards, measurement and individual performance is more elusive than one might initially assume.

Fourthly, pay-for-performance schemes often fail due to implementation difficulties and because the benefits of the implementation did not outweigh the costs. As we saw in Chapter 3, the cost of measurement can be considerable. Hewlett-Packard discovered this for themselves in the mid-to-late 1990s, when the complications of designing and maintaining an effective pay-for-performance programme in rapidly changing business circumstances meant that they trialled and then ditched several schemes.[21] Lantech, a manufacturer of packaging machinery in Louisville, Kentucky, found that the financial incentives given to individual employees caused intense and dysfunctional rivalry. The cost was not so much in the implementation of the system, but in the time spent on ironing out the issues between employees. Lantech's chairman has been quoted as saying "I was spending 95% of my time on conflict resolution instead of on how to serve our customers."[22] As with other measurement madness tales, pay-for-performance can lead to unintended consequences such as bad feelings, damaged relationships among colleagues and a lack of teamwork. An increasingly common view is that compensation is determined more by political skills and ingratiating personalities than by actual performance.[21]

Fifthly, while rewards can have an impact on people's actions and performance in the short term, they are ineffective at producing lasting changes in people's attitudes and behaviour. Financial incentives may in fact encourage the short-termism we described in the case of AIG FP, which is a powerful, but by no means isolated, illustration of the damages of rewarding short-term achievements at the expense of longer-term growth and sustainability.[23]

The discussion on pay-for-performance explains why financial rewards are often seen as an instrument for creating alignment and providing direction: the idea is that the agent will behave consistently with what is demanded by the principal. However, we have also seen that these same rewards come at a cost and could be blamed for failing to empower or generate commitment.[24] Echoing this, a recent article on performance-related pay in hospitals, which appeared in the *New York Times*, called the pay-for-performance provisions "a triumph of theory over experience".[25] In addition, although pay and rewards are important for people when they are considering a job offer, once they have joined the organization, pay will only be a hygiene factor; something that we come to expect and take for granted. In other words, you go to work because you are paid, but it doesn't motivate you to work harder.[26] Notably, such findings are consistent both in private companies and public sector organizations. Indeed, as we mentioned in previous chapters, the use of performance-related pay has rarely been found to improve the motivation of public servants.[27]

These last points are tightly connected to the very concept of motivation. In our discussion, we have emphasized the roles of measurement and rewards in influencing attitudes and behaviours, but are these effective "motivators"? Also, performance measures and rewards can focus our attention and efforts, but what are their impacts on performance? As the paragraphs above suggest, focusing people's attention does not automatically lead to enhanced performance. Although money may make us sit up and take notice, it does not necessarily motivate us. But what does? How can we use performance measurement systems to motivate people to achieve long-term goals?

WHAT MOTIVATES US?

What motivates us is a key question when we are concerned with performance measurement. As we have discussed throughout this book, performance measurement systems are primarily designed to influence behaviour and to motivate individuals to carry out tasks, which can contribute to an organization's success. Motivational factors can be categorized in various ways. In the 1960s, psychologist Frederick Hertzberg made the distinction between hygiene factors and motivators, arguing that what motivates people at work is not simply the opposite of what makes them dissatisfied.[28] Indeed, unhappiness at work might be down to a variety of reasons, such as a low salary, no window in the office or unsociable hours. However, just bringing someone's salary to the industry average, seating that person near a window and changing their work schedule will not motivate them to go the extra mile. These are things that one comes to expect as normal. Motivators, however, are very different; they are the factors that continuously push the individual to keep going and try harder.

The word motivation derives from the Latin "movere", meaning "to move"; therefore, to be motivated means "to be moved to do something".[29] We may be moved to do something either because we find it inherently interesting, enjoyable or valuable, which is known as *intrinsic motivation*; or because it leads to a desired outcome, such as a prize or a monetary reward, known as *extrinsic motivation*.[29] Intrinsic motivation is something that comes from within and extrinsic motivation is something that comes from outside. Although the two are not independent, they are quite different, and this is particularly evident when we look at the motivation of individuals and groups in the workplace.

Let us look at intrinsic and extrinsic motivation in relation to the use of measures and targets. Extrinsic motivation comes in four different guises. At the bottom end of the scale is the coldest form of extrinsic motivation, when we do something because we have to, when we do something solely to satisfy an external demand, to simply comply with some form of regulation, or to obtain an externally imposed reward. This is what we see when indicators are imposed by parent companies or regulators, but then are neither fully incorporated into the measurement system, nor properly communicated to the relevant individuals. The second level of extrinsic motivation manifests itself when we feel more involved and therefore do something because we see some personal benefit. It enhances our self-esteem and gives us a feeling of personal worth. In this case, the measurement system and rewards, if present, are more clearly connected to individuals and their roles, for example by being included in an individual's performance appraisal. At the next stage we find the situation where the individual has understood and endorsed certain goals or targets, and has intentionally decided to behave in a certain manner. This more proactive stance can be triggered by greater involvement in the process of setting indicators, targets and reward schemes. Finally, a higher level of motivation is achieved when goals and regulations have been fully assimilated, and they are perceived to be in congruence with one's own personal values and needs.[29] In other words, we are more motivated when we can see a clear line between organizational values, objectives, measurement systems and our own personal values. In addition, it has been shown that the more people understand the reasons for the goals and targets, the more the goals and targets will drive behaviour, and the more they will enable people to have autonomy and self-regulation[29] (see Table 9.1). If such understanding of company goals and targets is reached, this will reduce the likelihood of gaming and cheating - the greatest pitfalls of all.

Table 9.1 Levels of extrinsic motivation.

Compliance	We do something to satisfy an external demand, e.g., because of externally designed targets and indicators
Personal benefit	We do something because we see some personal benefit, e.g., through the introduction of objectives, targets and indicators in our performance appraisal
Personal involvement	We do something because we have understood and endorsed certain goals or targets, e.g., by being involved in their design and implementation
Congruence with personal values	We do something because we believe in the organization's values and goals, and regard the measurement system as a means to achieve them

Pure intrinsic motivation is an even higher form of motivation, as it is internally generated, and associated with interest, enjoyment, sense of competence and personal satisfaction: I do something because I want to. Whilst intrinsic and extrinsic motivations are not mutually exclusive, studies have shown an interesting, although potentially quite dangerous, relationship between the two. The introduction of extrinsic motivators may in fact have a negative effect on already established intrinsic motivation and commitment. The use of external incentives tends to decrease an individual's intrinsic motivation to perform a task.[30] In addition, the shift in motivation to extrinsic factors, such as financial rewards, ends up undermining pre-existing intrinsic motivation, so that people start assuming that they are doing something to achieve the reward, rather than to attain a wider organizational goal.[31]

Consider the scenario of asking your daughter to tidy her bedroom. If she is naturally tidy or she thinks that, being a member of the family, keeping the house in order is the right thing to do, then she will do so because of her own intrinsic motivation. Apparently such children do exist! If she needs a little encouragement, then praise and recognition of her efforts may well go a long way. However, consider the impact of offering a monetary reward instead. Once given, you will never be able to take the initial reward away, the intrinsic motivation will be gone and that bedroom will never be tidied again for free![32]

This point relates to another dysfunctional effect of rewards: once a reward is offered, it will be required and expected often in increasing amounts, for example your child may soon ask for a pay rise to keep their bedroom tidy. This has been shown in many contexts. For example, a recent article in the *Wall Street Journal* reported that American university students, who enjoyed playing with challenging puzzles, lost interest in spontaneous playing once they had been paid to solve them.[33]

A similar, more grown-up, example comes from a company that was renowned for valuing intrinsic motivation, coming fifth in the UK *Sunday Times* "Best Companies to Work For". However, there were also fantastic extrinsic rewards, one of which was the annual company party. This was no ordinary party: once a year all staff were taken on an all-expenses-paid trip abroad to celebrate in one of the European capitals. However, one year, after a fire in the Channel Tunnel had forced the cancellation of the planned jolly, the party was rearranged to take place in London. The entire five-star hotel costs were paid for, the entertainment was laid on and there were to be copious amounts of champagne. Given that the company was based 30 miles west of London, and that quite a few of the employees actually lived in London, the company told everyone that it was up to them how they arrived at the hotel, but on this occasion travel expenses would be down to the individual. You would not imagine the furore that this engendered. This is a clear example of initially receiving a reward and then requiring and expecting it ever after.[34]

Importantly, such a dysfunctional consequence is mostly determined by financial rewards, rather than by more informal rewards, such as praise, which can in fact increase intrinsic motivation. This effect of rewards and diminishing returns is not just confined to individuals in organizations, but can be found in all walks of life, from programmes aimed at helping people to lose weight or to stop smoking, to those initiatives encouraging people to wear seat belts. What is typically found is that, at the beginning, individuals who are extrinsically rewarded are more motivated than those who are not offered the reward. However, in the long run, they do not do as well as those who are purely intrinsically motivated, demonstrating that rewards have an impact in the short term, but not on engagement and in persistence in achieving a goal.[34] As David Russo, formerly head of human resources at SAS Institute, once commented "a raise is only a raise for 30 days. After that, it's just somebody's salary."[5]

Even more worryingly, research has shown that the more sophisticated and open-ended a task is, the worse people perform when working for a reward.[35] Let us take the example of open-source software developers. These are engineers who usually have a high-paying day job writing software. Then, in their spare time, they work collaboratively with other developers to write yet more software, but this time for no extrinsic reward. They do this because they enjoy the freedom and creativity that such a pastime delivers, not because of the lure of a big bonus. Do we believe that they show such enthusiasm during their working day? Research would say no. So, while financial rewards play an important role in focusing our attention, intrinsic rewards make us more open to experimentation and creativity.

LEARNING POINTS

In this chapter we have provided a critique of the use of rewards, especially financial rewards. Over the past decade the use of pay-for-performance schemes, especially for company executives, has risen to incredibly high levels. Pay and pay-for-performance schemes have proved positive for attracting and retaining people and for motivating individuals in the short term. However, evidence shows that in the medium to long term the impact of financial rewards on organizational performance is mostly negative, and that the link between pay and performance is ever more tenuous. Avoiding the costly mistakes of introducing pay-for-performance for the wrong reasons is paramount for preventing the madness described in this chapter.

Motivation and long-term goals

Research on motivation, in the workplace and elsewhere, has shown that there are a number of aspects to consider if you want to foster and sustain improvements in performance. There is no one-size-fits-all "recipe for success", but you can avoid motivational traps, and use measurement and rewards in a positive way.

In theory, one of the main reasons for introducing financial rewards is to align managers' actions with shareholders' interests and company objectives. Paradoxically, however, the main observable effect is that such rewards increase short-termism and personal benefit at the expense of the organization's interests. This is because financial rewards are often linked to short-term targets rather than to long-term goals. Also, before even considering measures, targets and rewards, you should bear in mind that, for individuals to succeed in their work, they need to feel competent; such a feeling of self-efficacy is connected to a desire for intellectual challenge and a desire to be better at what we do. Without it, it is very difficult to demand, or even generate, higher performance – with or without measures, targets and rewards.

Our open-source developers are motivated because they are working with equally intelligent and able engineers. Such teamwork can lead to improvement, both at the individual and the group levels, especially if accompanied by a sense of autonomy. After all, no one is directing them on how or when to write their code.[29] Notably, autonomy does not mean "do what you want"; rather, it means acting with choice. In an organizational context, this translates into willingly pursuing the company's objectives and respecting boundaries. Here, measurement and rewards, especially non-financial ones, can play a fundamental role, not as ways to prescribe and constrain, but as means to guide, support and provide feedback. This point was also raised in Chapter 6 in relation to target setting, where we considered the importance of using performance measurement systems as enabling rather than controlling mechanisms. In this case, we see that the effectiveness of a measurement system at the organizational level must also consider the individuals and their motivation.

Different strokes for different folks

Although rewards and measurement are full of pitfalls, the solution is not to automatically scrap all reward schemes. As mentioned earlier in this chapter, pay is not only a means to an end, but it is strongly connected to perceptions of social status and of personal accomplishment. Also, financial incentives do motivate people in the short term; they can provide information and focus behaviours; and they can give an appealing signal of competitiveness and recognition of individual effort and achievements to potential employees.

Rewards, especially individual financial rewards, amplify both the positive and the negative effects of measurement systems. Therefore, as much as it is possible to implement effective performance measurement systems, introducing "good" rewards is just as feasible, provided you move away from the popular view that people's performance is perfectly and objectively measurable, and that financial rewards are necessarily conducive to better performance.

To begin with, you should acknowledge that different things motivate different people: understanding what makes people tick is certainly a good investment of your time before you decide which type of reward to offer.[ii] Obviously no one would oppose the use of pay or bonuses. However, some people may find fair and adequate pay a necessity, and just want to concentrate on their work and take the issue of money off the table. Yet, others may find that extrinsic, financial rewards are all that matter.

However, rewards do not always have to be monetary: non-financial rewards, such as praise and positive feedback, and, to some extent, awards and honours, can be better extrinsic motivators than money. Indeed, such rewards might be some of the most powerful motivational tools available to you, so try to use them to their maximum effect.[4]

The right measures

Even advocates of pay-for-performance agree that identifying the right measures on which to base monetary rewards is difficult. Financial incentives work best when you have a good knowledge of the tasks and actions to be undertaken, when principals and agents have information that is largely similar, when you can separate out different individuals' performance, and when such individuals can control, to a good extent, what is being measured.

As we discussed in depth in Chapter 7, the more pressure you put on individuals and teams through performance measurement, the more likely they will be to game the system. Unfortunately, financial rewards tend to increase that pressure, and therefore the lessons taken from the gaming chapter doubly apply here.

[ii] It is also widely demonstrated that the effects of pay and rewards vary across national and organizational cultures, between genders, etc.

The time to reward

Contrary to the idea that rewards should be discussed up front in order to incentivize workers, one school of thought is that rewards may work better when they are unexpected and offered only after a task is complete.[36] Such an arrangement would not only lessen the negative effects of using extrinsic rewards, but it might also increase individuals' intrinsic motivation. In addition, *post factum* rewards are more likely to reinforce a sense of achievement and, possibly, the pride of belonging to a team or an organization. However, this would also mean that such rewards used in combination with targets would reduce goal clarity, as seen in Chapter 6.

Team vs. individual rewards

Rewards should not necessarily be given to individuals. Although this is the predominant assumption and focus of reward schemes, it has been shown that team-based incentives may be much more effective. One of the reasons you may wish to consider team rewards is that you are more able to assess performance reliably if you use an aggregated unit of performance. If you are assessing a project team, it is often difficult to separate out who was specifically responsible for what, and what each individual contribution was worth to the overall success of the team.[37] Another reason is that the collaboration of individuals and teams is an important aspect of work and a key means of improving performance. If you try to differentiate the performance of individuals, you may well find that you penalize teamwork, which will then lead to worse results overall.[21] The last thing you would want to do is increase the risk of dysfunctional competition among employees, which, as in the case of sales executives, could result in price wars and an overall decrease in margins. On the other hand, we should always try to minimize the free rider problem, which arises when we shift the focus from the individual to the team.

Lastly, finding our job inherently interesting, enjoyable or valuable is a much more potent engine for learning and improvement than the use of carrot and stick mechanisms. This engine will be even stronger if you give people the opportunity to improve their abilities and skills, if they perceive themselves as capable of doing their job, if they can act with choice, and if they feel part of a wider system where their values are aligned with the ones of their organizations. By the same token, extrinsic rewards may actually supplant intrinsic motivation, sometimes forever. Therefore, if you are lucky enough to work with people who have this potent engine of intrinsic motivation, you might be better served helping them sustain and develop it rather than introduce a system of external rewards.

AND FINALLY...

Opponents of the use of financial incentives have argued that these tools perpetuate the fundamental human tendency of being "unrealistically optimistic about what can be accomplished by a management intervention".[21] According to these commentators, financial rewards can harm organizations' long-term performance by destroying intrinsic motivation and narrowing people's focus on the attainment of the reward, rather than on the organization's objectives. Furthermore, rewards can provide signals that are too blunt; they can promote the wrong behaviours; and they can attract the wrong kind of talent. Looking at the link between rewards and motivation, Alfie Kohn sarcastically stated: "Do rewards motivate people? Absolutely. They motivate people to get rewards."[35] Or, as Stanford Professor Jeffrey Pfeffer stated:

> People do work for money – but they work even more for meaning in their lives. In fact, they work to have fun. Companies that ignore this fact are essentially bribing their employees and will pay the price in a lack of loyalty and commitment.[37]

PART

IV

Conclusions

10

Will Measurement Madness Ever be Cured?

Measuring for the sake of measuring, comparing the incomparable and hoping for improvement whilst rewarding failure are some of the key measurement pitfalls exposed in this book. We have discussed the multiplicity of reasons that drive organizations to measure, delved into the complexities of performance measurement and demonstrated that, although well intentioned, management efforts often result in measurement madness. Despite the antidotes we prescribed at the end of each chapter to help prevent or at least alleviate the dysfunctional consequences of measurement efforts, the question remains: can such madness ever be cured?

All organizations, however small, are complex organisms made up of complex human beings with their own individual habits, preferences, skills, knowledge, emotions and aspirations. Measuring and managing performance is a profoundly social activity, which is tightly linked to the behaviours of individuals and groups. In our work with organizations, we are often faced with the situation where the search for "the right measures" inevitably leads to questions about the overall direction of the organization, its strategy, the organizational culture and the behaviours these three elements engender. We hope that the stories we have recounted demonstrate that performance measurement is not a "neutral" activity, but that it is intimately related to how people behave and act. Indeed, if we were to summarize the message of this book in a sentence, it would simply be this: "Measures will *always* change behaviour, and your troubles will start the moment you forget this." Remembering this simple fact should help you and your organization avoid becoming one of the stories in our next book.

Performance measurement is, of course, constantly developing, and advances in technology, business models and networks are taking us into new and uncharted waters. The biggest changes, which we have seen in recent years, are: the use of performance measurement across organizational boundaries, for example throughout the supply chain; and the increasing use of business analytics under the umbrella of "Big Data". What might these changes mean for recognizing and avoiding performance measurement pitfalls? Will "shared" performance measurement help organizations overcome the difficulties illustrated by our stories? Will "Big Data" render obsolete many of the issues described in this book? Desirable as it would be, we do not believe that either of these scenarios is likely to be a cure for measurement madness.

Whether it is because we want to have more integrated supply chains, or aim for greater synergies between companies, or promote collaborative work to impact social outcomes, measuring performance across organizations is certainly a positive development. However, the word of warning is that it can introduce additional complexity into what is already a thick web of competing agendas, conflicting interests and multiple priorities. Extending performance measurement efforts to cover multiple organizations brings with it additional issues of data ownership, varying standards and data definitions, different IT systems and, of course, more people. If avoiding the pitfalls of performance measurement starts with thinking through and recognizing the behavioural consequences of measurement, the difficulty of this in a multi-organizational setting is manifestly increased.

"Big Data" is also a very welcome development, promising to process ever larger quantities of data, from variable sources, ever more quickly and thereby enabling an organization, through the use of mathematical algorithms, to find patterns and relationships that would be otherwise impossible to discover. The promised advantages are many, from reducing costs to improving the quality of products and services, to identifying new customer segments or uncovering hidden societal needs. And once we have the data, there is no need to worry about anything else, right?

Unfortunately, the promise of minimizing the "human element" in performance measurement and providing objective insight through hard data and sophisticated analytical tools is largely unfounded. The problem with "Big Data", as we see it, is that far from substituting behavioural issues, it amplifies them. No amount of data processing can provide a substitute for clarity of thinking and a concern about the impact of measurement on people. Also, analyzing larger volumes of data may mean including unreliable external datasets and, therefore, decreasing data reliability; potentially disconnecting data and the business processes and people they are supposed to support; and basing decision-making processes on data that may be scarcely comprehensible, but nevertheless treated as authoritative. In a recent survey of retailers, for example, respondents said they couldn't analyze data at a low enough level of detail, and that reporting tools couldn't handle the level of sophistication of the questions being asked of the data.[i] We also think, more importantly, that the ability to analyze and examine so many data points may mask what is important,[ii] whilst at the same time giving us the impression that we can manage resources and processes in a purely mechanical way. If so, bigger data could well lead to ever greater madness!

Does all this mean that we should not share data between organizations, forget about technological developments and, ultimately, oppose any form of measurement? Of course not. Effective performance measurement is still possible and the pitfalls described herein can be avoided. Returning to our opening story about Mike, before embarking on their "Performance Excellence" journey, Mike's company was experiencing problems that are common to almost all organizations: insufficient understanding of the company's main performance drivers and of current performance; silo mentality and limited collaboration between functions; and lack of clarity about the organization's goals. As we have discussed in each of the chapters' learning points, well-designed and implemented performance measurement systems can be of great assistance in each of these areas, and performance measures can help establish an organization's position, enhance clarity around goals, processes and roles, and align behaviours with the organization's strategy.

However, Mike's main mistake was to assume that good infrastructure and sufficient resources would automatically lead to such improvements. This is not uncommon: we often see dedicated departments tasked with performance measurement and job titles such as "Performance Manager", "Performance and Quality Officer" or "Change and Improvement Manager". Whilst appointing someone to coordinate the identification of performance drivers and designing targets and indicators is often good practice, performance measurement is a deeply social process: everyone in an organization is involved in and affected by it, at least in capturing, reporting and using performance data.

---

[i] Read more: The problem with "Big Data" – FierceRetailIT http://www.fierceretail .com/retailit/story/problem-big-data/2014-03-19#ixzz31nQ8CImp

[ii] See Glenn Greenwald's discussion in his book *No Place to Hide: Edward Snowden, the NSA and the Surveillance State* on the challenges faced by the security services in identifying the real terrorist threats from all the data on ordinary people.

AND FINALLY...

Many years ago, Armand Feigenbaum, one of the fathers of the Quality Management movement, reputedly said that "quality is everybody's job", meaning that every person in an organization can affect the quality of its products and services. We believe that "performance" is also everybody's job – perhaps even more so than quality – and that performance measurement is a process that touches on everyone and permeates all organizational activities. Keeping this in mind will help you steer clear of the performance measurement pitfalls described in this book.

REFERENCES

CHAPTER 2

1. Franco-Santos, M., Lucianetti, L. and Bourne, M. (2012) Contemporary performance measurement systems: a review of their consequences and a framework for research, *Management Accounting Research*, 23(2), 79–119.
2. Based on Mari, L. (2007) Measurability, in Boumans M. (Ed.), *Measurement in Economics*. London: Elsevier; and Micheli, P. and Mari, L. (2014) The theory and practice of performance measurement, *Management Accounting Research*, 25(2), June, 147–156.
3. Franco-Santos, M., Kennerley, M., Micheli, P., Martinez, V., Mason, S., Marr, B., Gray, D. and Neely, A. (2007) Towards a definition of a business performance measurement system, *International Journal of Operations and Production Management*, 27(8), 784–801.
4. Chwastiak, M. (2006) Rationality, performance measures and representations of reality: planning, programming and budgeting and the Vietnam war, *Critical Perspectives on Accounting*, 17(1), 29–55.
5. Micheli, P. and Manzoni, J.-F. (2010) Strategic performance measurement: benefits, limitations and paradoxes, *Long Range Planning*, 43(4), 465–476.
6. Delmas, M., Etzion, D. and Nairn-Birch, N. (2013) Triangulating environmental performance: what do corporate social responsibility ratings really capture? *Academy of Management Perspectives*, 27(3), 255–267; p. 263.

CHAPTER 3

1. McAfee, A. and Brynjolfsson, E. (2012) Big Data: the management revolution, *Harvard Business Review*, October, 60–68.
2. Kiron D. and Shockley R. (2011) Creating business values with analytics, *MIT Sloan Management Review*, 53(1), 57–63.
3. Ambler, T. (2003) *Marketing and the Bottom Line*, 2nd ed., Harlow: Pearson Education Limited, p. 6.
4. Smith, P. (1995) On the unintended consequences of publishing performance data in the public sector, *International Journal of Public Administration*, 18, 277–310.

5. Smith, R. (2012) Doctors to launch investigation into Liverpool Care Pathway, *The Telegraph*, 24 Oct, online at http://www.telegraph.co.uk/health/healthnews/9630194/Doctors-to-launch-investigation-into-Liverpool-Care-Pathway.html.

6. Barrett, D. (2013) Police chief admits crime figures "adjusted", *The Daily Telegraph*, 21 November, 1, National 8.

7. Vogel, S. (2012) VA mental health system sharply denounced at hearing: the Department of Veterans Affairs' mental health-care system focuses more on meeting performance goals than helping veterans, critics told a Senate hearing, *WashingtonPost.com*, 26 April.

8. Neely, A., Sutcliff, M.R., and Heyns, H.R. (2001) Driving Value through Strategic Planning and Budgeting, *A Research Report from Cranfield School of Management and Accenture*, online at http://www.som.cranfield.ac.uk/som/dinamic-content/media/CBP/Areas%20of%20Expertise/Neely%20A%20Sutcliff%20MR%20Heyns%20HR%20-%202001%20-%20Driving%20Value%20Through%20Strategic%20Planning%20and%20Budgeting.pdf.

9. Morgan, C. (2003) Measuring performance: supply-chain challenge, *Focus*, March, 44–46.

10. Kaplan, R. and Norton, D. (2004) *Strategy Maps: Converting Intangible Assets into Tangible Outcomes*, Harvard Business Review Press.

11. Neely, A., Adams, C. and Kennerly, M. (2002) *The Performance Prism: The Scorecard for Measuring and Managing Business Success*, Financial Times Prentice Hall.

CHAPTER 4

1. See, for instance, the 2013 Road Safety Annual Report published by the International Transport Forum (http://www.internationaltransportforum.org/irtadpublic/pdf/13IrtadReport.pdf); the Violence and Injury Prevention Programme run by the World Health Organization (http://www.who.int/violence_injury_prevention/en/); and The 2013 Definitions, Sources, and Methods document compiled by the OECD.

2. Neely, A., Richards, H., Mills, J., Platts, K. and Bourne, M. (1997) Designing performance measures: a structured approach, *International Journal of Operations and Production Management*, 17(11), 1131–1152.

3. Callioni, G., de Montgros, X., Slagmulder, R., Van Wassenhove, L.N. and Wright, L. (2005) Inventory-driven costs, *Harvard Business Review*, 83(3), 135–141.

4. Reilly, A. (2013) CEO Statement to the Joint Oireachtas Committee on Agriculture, Food and the Marine, *Food Safety Authority of Ireland* (http://www.fsai.ie/news_centre/oireachtas_05.02.2013.html).
5. Neely, A., Adams, C. and Kennerley, M. (2002) *The Performance Prism*, Edinburgh: Pearson Education.
6. Mars Climate Orbiter Mishap Investigation Board Phase I Report (press release), NASA, November 10, 1999. Retrieved February 22, 2013 (http://sunnyday.mit.edu/accidents/MCO_report.pdf).
7. Public Service Productivity Estimates: Healthcare 2004.
8. BBC News (2004) NHS is 'wasteful and inefficient', 19 Oct, online at http://news.bbc.co.uk/1/hi/health/3755438.stm.
9. National Audit Office (2006) PSA Target: Performance Information. A survey report on the views of departmental Finance Directors and PSA Target Owners on working with Public Service Agreements, London: Her Majesty's Stationery Office, online at http://www.nao.org.uk/wp-content/uploads/2006/04/Acting_on_Information.pdf.

CHAPTER 5

1. Slack, N., Chambers, S., and Johnston, R. (2010) *Operations Management*, 6th ed., Harlow, England: Pearson Education, 401–404.
2. Bottle, A. and Aylin, P (2006) Mortality associated with delay in operation after hip fracture: observational study, *British Medical Journal*, 332, 947.
3. Department for Transport (2008) Road casualties. Great Britain 2007 Annual Report. London.
4. Institute and Faculty of Actuaries (2012) Report on third party motor claims and periodic payment orders.
5. Key to the University Statistics Table", *Push.co.uk*, online at http://www.push.co.uk/Key-to-the-university-statistics-table.
6. Bosio, A and Disney, R (2011) Public Sector Pay and Pensions in *The IFS Green Budget: February 2011*, The Institute for Fiscal Studies, online at http://www.ifs.org.uk/budgets/gb2011/11chap7.pdf.
7. *Reclaiming the Sceptic* (2012) Radio Programme, BBC Radio 4, London, 11 July, 2012.
8. Deacon, M. (2013) Sketch: Michael Gove's Pisa delivery, *The Telegraph*, 3 Dec, online at http://www.telegraph.co.uk/news/politics/10491563/Sketch-Michael-Goves-Pisa-delivery.html.

9. Clark, L. (2012) Major universities reveal explosion in student cheating over the last three years, *Mail Online*, 2 Mar, online at http://www.dailymail.co.uk/news/article-2109527/Major-universities-reveal-explosion-student-cheating-years.html.
10. Cialdini, R.B., Borden, R.J., Thorne, A., Walker, M.R., Freeman, S. and Sloan, L.R. (1976) Basking in reflected glory: three (football) field studies, *Journal of Personality and Social Psychology*, 34, 366–375.
11. Hutchens, G. (2013) Bosses incentive schemes guided by herd mentality, *The Sydney Morning Herald*, 12th January, First, 7.
12. Watt, H., Newell, C., Winnett, R., Patton, G. (2011) Exam boards: how examiners tip off teachers to help students pass, *The Telegraph*, online at http://www.telegraph.co.uk/education/secondaryeducation/8940781/Exam-boards-how-examiners-tip-off-teachers-to-help-students-pass.html.
13. McKee, M. and Hunter, D. (1995) Mortality league tables: do they inform or mislead? *Quality Health Care*, 4, 5–12.

CHAPTER 6

1. *The Guardian* (2009) Thursday 19th March, London.
2. *The Daily Telegraph* (2011) World's Hottest Chilli Contest Leaves Two in Hospital, 5th October, online at http://www.telegraph.co.uk/foodanddrink/foodanddrinknews/8808120/Worlds-hottest-chilli-contest-leaves-two-in-hospital.html.
3. Franco, M. and Bourne, M. (2008) The impact of performance targets on behaviour: a close look at sales force contexts, Report prepared for the *Chartered Institute of Management Accountants*, UK.
4. Locke, E.A., Shaw, K.N., Saari, L.M. and Latham, G.P. (1981) Goal setting and task performance: 1969–1980, *Psychological Bulletin*, 90, 125–152.
5. Ordonez, L., Schweitzer, M.E., Galinsky, A. and Bazerman, M. (2009) Goals gone wild: how goals systematically harm individuals and organizations, *Academy of Management Perspectives*, 23(1), 6–16.
6. Caulkin, S. (2009) "This isn't an abstract problem. Targets can kill", *The Observer*, 22 March, online at http://www.theguardian.com/business/2009/mar/22/policy.
7. BBC News (2014) Stafford Hospital timeline, 24th February 2014, online at http://www.bbc.co.uk/news/uk-england-stoke-staffordshire-20965469.
8. Advani, R. (2006) *The Wall Street MBA: Your Personal Crash Course in Corporate Finance.* New York: McGraw-Hill.

9. Jensen, M. (2003) Paying people to lie: the truth about the budgeting process, *European Financial Management*, 9(3), 379–406.

10. Kelman, S. and Friedman, J.N. (2009) Performance improvement and performance dysfunction: an empirical examination of distortionary impacts of the emergency room wait-time target in the English National Health Service, *Journal of Public Administration Research and Theory*, 19, 917–946.

11. Propper, C., Sutton, M., Whitnall, C. and Windmeijer, F. (2010) Incentives and targets in hospital care: evidence from a natural experiment, *Journal of Public Economics*, 94(3–4), 318–335.

12. The office of the President Elect, online at http://change.gov/agenda/ ethics_agenda/.

13. Micheli, P. and Neely, A. (2010) Performance measurement in the English public sector: Searching for the golden thread, *Public Administration Review*, 70(4), 591–600.

14. Greenwood, C. (2013) How violent crimes 'are made to vanish like a puff of smoke': Police chiefs tell MPs that stats are routinely fiddled, *The Daily Mail*, 20th November, online at http://www.dailymail.co.uk/news/ article-2510048/Police-chiefs-tell-MPs-stats-routinely-fiddled.html.

15. Dodd, V. and Rawlinson, K. (2013) Police fail to investigate rapes and child abuse, Commons committee is told, *The Guardian*, 19th November, online at http://www.theguardian.com/uk-news/2013/nov/19/police-failures-rape-child-abuse-official-statistics.

16. Babchuk, N. and Goode, W. (1951) Work incentives in a self-determined work group, *American Social Review*, 16, 679–687.

17. Hawkes, S. and Armstrong, A. (2013) Lloyds fined £28m for 'sell or be demoted' incentive plan, *The Daily Telegraph*, 11 December, online at http://www.telegraph.co.uk/finance/newsbysector/banksandfinance/ 10510228/Lloyds-fined-28m-for-sell-or-be-demoted-incentive-plan.html.

18. Collinson, P. (2013) Lloyds has failed to learn the lessons of previous mis-selling fines, *The Guardian*, 11th December, online at http://www. theguardian.com/business/2013/dec/11/lloyds-bank-failed-mis-selling-fines.

19. Seijts, G. and Latham, G. (2005) Learning versus performance goals: when should each be used? *Academy of Management Executive*, 19(1), 124–131; p. 124.

20. Loomis, C. (2003) The whistleblower and the CEO, *Fortune*, 7 July, pp. 88-96.

21. Voreacos, D. and Kharif, O. (2010) Alcatel-Lucent to pay $137 million in bribe probes, *Bloomberg*, 28th December.

22. Berliner, Joseph S. (1956) A problem in soviet business management, *Administrative Science Quarterly*, 1, 86–101.

23. Carvel, J. (2003) reported in Kelman, S. and Friedman, J.N. (2009) Performance improvement and performance dysfunction: an empirical examination of distortionary impacts of the emergency room wait-time in the English National Health Service, *Journal of Public Administration Research and Theory*, 19, 917–946; p. 918.

24. Steven Kelman and John N. Friedman (2009) Performance Improvement and Performance Dysfunction: An Empirical Examination of Distortionary Impacts of the Emergency Room Wait-Time Target in the English National Health Service, *Journal of Public Administration Research and Theory* (2009) 19(4): pp. 917–946 by permission of Oxford University Press on behalf of the *Journal of Public Administration Research and Theory*, Inc. All rights reserved.

25. Seddon, J. (2008) *Systems Thinking in the Public Sector*, Axminster, UK: Triarchy Press.

26. Meekings, A., Briault, S. and Neely, A. (2011) How to avoid the problems of target-setting, *Performance Measurement Association newsletter*, 8(2), 10–14.

27. Royal Statistical Society (2005) *Performance indicators: Good, bad and ugly* (http://www.rss.org.uk/uploadedfiles/documentlibrary/739.pdf; 26–27).

28. Hall, M. (2008) The effect of comprehensive performance measurement systems on role clarity, psychological empowerment and managerial performance, *Accounting, Organizations and Society*, 33(2–3), 141–163.

29. Melnyk, S.A., Hanson, J. and Calantone, R. (2010) Hitting the target... but missing the point: resolving the paradox of strategic transition, *Long Range Planning*, 43(4), 555–74, for the original discussion of this case.

30. Reported in Metzenbaum, S. (2009) *Performance Management Recommendations for the New Administration*, IBM Center for the Business of Government, p. 34.

31. Locke, E.A. and Latham, G.P. (2006) New directions in goal-setting theory, *Current Directions in Psychological Science*, 15(5), 265–268; p. 265.

32. Gimbert, X., Bisbe, J. and Mendoza, X. (2010) The role of performance measurement systems in strategy formulation processes, *Long Range Planning*, 43(4), 477–497.

33. Milkovich, G.T., Wigdor, A.K. (1991) *Pay for Performance*. Washington, DC: National Academy Press; p. 85

34. Locke, E. A. (2004) Linking goals to monetary incentives, *Academy of Management Executive*, 18(4): 130-133.
35. Latham, G. (2004) The motivational benefits of goal-setting, *Academy of Management Executive*, 18(4), 126–129.

CHAPTER 7

1. Otley, D.T. (2003) Management control and performance management: whence and whither? *British Accounting Review*, 35(4), 309–326.
2. Hope, C. (2013) David Cameron: Tax avoiding foreign firms like Starbucks and Amazon lack 'moral scruples'. *The Daily Telegraph*, 04 Jan, online at http://www.telegraph.co.uk/news/politics/david-cameron/9779983/David-Cameron-Tax-avoiding-foreign-firms-like-Starbucks-and-Amazon-lack-moral-scruples.html#.
3. Cowie, I. (2013) Top tax dodgers – including 'green fraudsters' – jailed for 150 years, *The Telegraph Blogs,* 04 Jan, online at http://blogs.telegraph.co.uk/finance/ianmcowie/100022028/top-tax-dodgers-including-green-fraudsters-jailed-for-150-years/.
4. Fisher, C. and Downes, B. (2008) Performance measurement and metric manipulation in the public sector, *Business Ethics: A European Review*, 17(3), 245–258.
5. Hailstone, L. (2011) VOSA targets magnet tacho cheats, Road Transport (www.roadtransport.com).
6. Alexander, R. (2012) Which is the world's biggest employer? *BBC News Magazine*, 20 Mar, online at http://www.bbc.co.uk/news/magazine-17429786.
7. National Audit Office (2001) Inappropriate Adjustments to NHS Waiting Lists. London: Her Majesty's Stationery Office. HC452. Online at http://www.nao.org.uk/publications/nao_reports/01-02/0102452.pdf.
8. Pitches, D., Burls, A. and Fry-Smith, A. (2003) Snakes, ladders, and spin: how to make a silk purse from a sow's ear – a comprehensive review of strategies to optimise data for corrupt managers and incompetent clinicians, *British Medical Journal*, 327.
9. Figlio, D.N. and Getzler, L.S. (2002) Accountability, ability, and disability: gaming the system, *NBER working paper 9307*; Cullen, J.B. and Reback, R. (2006) Tinkering towards accolades: school gaming under a performance accountability system, *Advances in Applied Microeconomics*, 14.

10. Severson, K. (2013) First trial ends in acquittal in school scandal in Atlanta, *The New York Times*, 7th September, Late Ed., p. 15.

11. Woods, D. (2011) Staff engage in behaviour to make sure they are paid for time not worked, global Kronos survey shows, *HR Magazine* online.

12. Myers, D. (2011) Workers being paid for time not worked, *CMI* online.

13. McGregor, J. (2014) Ethical misconduct, by the numbers, *WashingtonPost .com*, 5th February.

14. *BBC News* (2008) Drug-free sport is Utopia – Rogge, 24 Nov, online at http://news.bbc.co.uk/sport1/hi/olympic_games/7747181.stm.

15. *FoxNews* (2012) Lance Armstrong stripped of all 7 Tour de France titles, banned for life, *FoxNews.com*, 22 Oct, online at http://www.foxnews.com/sports/2012/10/22/decision-day-for-lance-armstrong/.

16. Le Grand, J. (2003) *Motivation, Agency, and Public Policy: Of Knights and Knaves, Pawns and Queens*, Oxford University Press, New York.

17. Cooper, H. (2014) 92 Air Force Officers Suspended for Cheating on Their Missile Exam. *The New York Times*, 30 Jan, online at http://www.nytimes.com/2014/01/31/us/politics/92-air-force-officers-suspended-for-cheating-on-their-missile-exam.html.

18. McGregor, J. (2013) The danger of how we grade teachers and schools. Take an overly simplistic set of measurements, add monetary rewards, throw in human failings, and you have a recipe for gaming the education system, *WashingtonPost.com*, 7th April 2013.

19. Barrett, D. (2013) Police chief admits crime figures "adjusted", *The Daily Telegraph*, 21st November, 1, National 8.

20. Buffett, W. (2003) Letter to shareholders of Berkshire Hathaway, 2002 Annual Report (Emphasis in the original).

21. Jenkins, C. (2011) University of Wales degree and visa scam exposed by BBC, 5th October 2011.

22. *BBC News* (2012) Rayat London College in Uni of Wales probe liquidated, 8 Mar, online at http://www.bbc.co.uk/news/uk-wales-17305360.

23. Goodhart, C. (1984) *Monetary Theory and Practice: The UK Experience*, Macmillan: London (NB: p. 94; cited in Bevan and Hood (2006) p. 521).

24. Van Yperen, N., Hamstra, M. and van der Klauw, M. (2011) To win, or not to lose, at any cost: the impact of achievement goals on cheating, *British Journal of Management*, 22, S5–S15.

25. Anderman, E.M. and Midgey, C. (2004) Changes in self-reported academic cheating across the transition from middle school to high school, *Contemporary Educational Psychology*, 29, 499–517, cited in Van Yperen, N., Hamstra, M. and van der Klauw, M. (2011) (p. S13).

26. Edelman, B. and Larkin, I. (2009) Demographics, career concerns or social comparison: who games SSRN download counts? *Harvard Business School Working Paper*, 09–096, February 2009.
27. Radnor, Z. (2008) "Muddled, massaging, manoeuvring or manipulated? A typology of organisational gaming." *International Journal of Productivity and Performance Management*, 15(4), 316–328.
28. Carnegy, G. and Wolnizer, P. (1996) "Enabling accountability in museums". *Accounting, Auditing and Accountability Journal*, 9(5), 84–99.
29. Hood, C. (2006) Gaming in Targetworld: the targets approach to managing British public services, *Public Administration Review*, July/August, 515–521.
30. De Bruijn, H. (2002) Performance measurement in the public sector: strategies to cope with the risks of performance measurement, *International Journal of Public Sector Management*, 15(7), 578–594.
31. Micheli, P. and Pavlov, A. (2008) Promoting a culture of performance management in public sector organizations. Holy Grail or achievable quest? *International Perspectives on Public Sector Performance Management*, KPMG.
32. Evans, M. (2013) Police told to use commonsense, *The Daily Telegraph*, 1, National, 11.
33. Keller, B. (2013) Carrots for doctors, *NYTimes.com Feed*, 28th January.
34. *BBC News* (2007) Clerks "told to manipulate cases", 03 Dec, online at http://news.bbc.co.uk/1/hi/england/shropshire/7125784.stm.

CHAPTER 8

1. Kerr, S. (1975) On the folly of rewarding A while hoping for B, *Academy of Management Journal*, 18(4), 769–783.
2. Jarrett, M. (2013) When CEOs Should Let It Be, *INSEAD Blog*, 15 Nov, INSEAD Knowledge.
3. Smith, P. (1995) On the unintended consequences of publishing performance data in the public sector, *International Journal of Public Administration*, 18(2–3), 277–310.
4. Curth, K. (2013) TN labor development dept. rewarded despite overspending $73M, television programme, WSMV Channel 4, Nashville, TN, 16 May, online at http://wsmv.membercenter.worldnow.com/story/22264933/tn-labor-development-dept-rewarded-despite-overspending-73m.

5. Martin, S. (2013) Customer continuity: Why change can be a bad thing, *British Airways Business Life Magazine*, 27 June, online at http://businesslife.ba.com/Ideas/Trends/Customer-continuity-why-change-can-be-a-bad-thing.html. See more about this topic at www.influenceatwork.co.uk.
6. Brachhi, P. and North, N. (2014) Ambulance queues at A&E and the deadly 999 lottery: Patients dying after four-hour waits as fleets of ambulances sit outside hospitals while others die waiting for the same crews to reach them, *Mail Online*, 1 Feb, online at http://www.dailymail.co.uk/news/article-2549931/Ambulance-queues-A-E-deadly-999-lottery-Patients-dying-four-hour-waits-fleets-ambulances-sit-outside-hospitals-die-waiting-crews-reach-them.html.

CHAPTER 9

1. Treanor, J. (2011) RBS report: regulators need new rules to crack down when banks go bust, *The Guardian*, 9th December, online at http://www.theguardian.com/business/2011/dec/09/rbs-report-regulators-banks-fsa.
2. *BBC News* (2011) RBS woes caused by poor decisions, says FSA, 12th December, online at http://www.bbc.co.uk/news/business-16135247.
3. *BBC News* (2012) Former RBS boss Fred Goodwin stripped of knighthood, 31st January, online at http://www.bbc.co.uk/news/uk-politics-16821650.
4. Hope, J. and Player, S. (2012) *Beyond Performance Management*, Boston, MA: Harvard Business Review Press, p. 348.
5. Pfeffer, J. and Sutton, R. (2006) *Hard Facts, Dangerous Half-Truths & Total Nonsense: Profiting from Evidence-Based Management*, Boston, MA: Harvard Business Review Press.
6. Jensen, M. and Murphy, K. (1990) CEO incentives – it's not how much you pay, but how, *Harvard Business Review*, May–June, pp. 138–149.
7. *BBC News* (2011) Powerful shareholder group ABI urges bank pay curbs, 6th December, online at http://www.bbc.co.uk/news/business-16043792.
8. *BBC News* (2011) Directors' pay rose 50% in past year, says IDS report, 28th October, online at http://www.bbc.co.uk/news/business-15487866.
9. *BBC News* (2011) Bosses' bonuses up by 187% since 2002, report suggests, 5th September, online at http://www.bbc.co.uk/news/business-14781254.
10. Taibbi, M. (2009) The big takeover: how Wall Street insiders are using the bailout to stage a revolution, *Rolling Stone*, 22nd March 2009.

11. Heineman, B.W. (2009) AIG's bonuses: A dangerous failure of leadership, *Harvard Business Review*, 19th March (http://blogs.hbr.org/cs/2009/03/perilous_obfuscation_aigs_bonu.html).

12 Rajan, Raghuram G. (2005) Has financial development made the world riskier, Paper presented at The Greenspan Era: Lessons for the Future Federal Reserve Bank of Kansas Symposium, Jackson Hole, WY.

13. Ledwith, M. (2012) Bring performance-related pay into the classroom say MPs as they target bad teachers, *The Daily Mail*, 1st May, online at http://www.dailymail.co.uk/news/article-2137684/Bad-teachers-paid-best-say-MPs.html.

14. http://www.publications.parliament.uk/pa/cm201012/cmselect/cmeduc/1515/151502.htm.

15. Griffiths, M. (2012) Performance-related pay fails the test for teachers, *The Guardian*, 1st May, online at http://www.theguardian.com/commentisfree/2012/may/01/performance-related-pay-teachers.

16. Intravaia, S. (2012) Valutazione delle scuole, questa volta il progetto del ministro ha fatto centro, *La Repubblica*, 29th March, online at http://www.repubblica.it/scuola/2012/03/29/news/presidi_progetto_vales-32356520/.

17. Rynes, S.L., Gerhart, B. and Minette, K.A. (2004) The importance of pay in employee motivation: discrepancies between what people say and what they do, *Human Resource Management*, 43(4), 381–394.

18. Shearer, Bruce S. (2004) Piece rates, fixed wages and incentives: evidence from a field experiment, *Review of Economic Studies*, 71(2), 513–534.

19. Rynes, S.L., Gerhart, B. and Parks, L. (2005) Personnel psychology: performance evaluation and pay for performance, *Annual Review of Psychology*, 56, 571–600; p. 582.

20. Bebchuk, L.A. and Fried, J.M. (2006) Pay without performance: overview of the issues, *Academy of Management Perspectives*, 20(1), 5–24.

21. Beer, M. and Cannon, M.D. (2004) Promise and peril in implementing pay-for-performance, *Human Resource Management*, 43(1), 3–48.

22. Pfeffer J. (1998) Six dangerous myths about pay, *Harvard Business Review*, 76(3), 108–20; p. 115.

23. Schwartz, N.D. and Silver-Greenberg, J. (2012) JPMorgan's trading loss is said to rise at least 50%, *The New York Times*, 16th May, online at http://dealbook.nytimes.com/2012/05/16/jpmorgans-trading-loss-is-said-to-rise-at-least-50/.

24. Argyris, C. (1992), *On Organizational Learning*. Blackwell Publishing: Cambridge, MA.

25. Keller, B. (2013) Carrots for doctors, *NYTimes.com Feed*, 28th January.
26. Rynes, S.L., Gerhart, B. and Minette, K.A. (2004) The importance of pay in employee motivation: Discrepancies between what people say and what they do, *Human Resource Management*, 43(4), 381–394.
27. Marsden, D. (2009) The paradox of performance related pay systems: Why do we keep adopting them in the face of evidence that they fail to motivate?, in Hood, C. and Margetts, H., *Paradoxes of modernization: unintended consequences of public policy reforms*, Oxford, UK: Oxford University Press.
28. Hertzberg, F. (2003) One more time: How do you motivate employees?, *Harvard Business Review*, Jan-Feb, 87–96; p. 87
29. Ryan, R. and Deci, E. (2000) Intrinsic and extrinsic motivations: Classic definitions and new directions, *Contemporary Educational Psychology*, 25, 54–67.
30. Deci, E. quoted in Pink, D. (2009) *Drive: The Surprising Truth About What Motivates Us*. London: Canongate Books Ltd, p. 8.
31. Aronson, E., Akert, R.D. and Wilson, T.D. (2006). *Social psychology* (6th ed.). Upper Saddle River, NJ: Pearson Prentice Hall.
32. Pink, D. (2009) *Drive: The Surprising Truth About What Motivates Us*, London: Canongate Books Ltd, p. 8.
33. Woolhandler, S. (2013) No: the system is too easy to game – and too hard to set up, in Big issues in health care (a special report) – should physician pay be tied to performance? *The Wall Street Journal*, 17th June, J, R2.
34. Bernabou, R. and Tirole, J. (2003) Intrinsic and extrinsic motivation, *Review of Economic Studies*, 70, 489–520, p. 503.
35. Kohn, A. (1993) Why incentive plans cannot work, *Harvard Business Review*, 71(5), 54–63; p. 55.
36. Hope, J. and Fraser, R. (2003) New ways of setting rewards: the beyond budgeting model, *California Management Review*, 45(4), 104–119; p. 109.
37. Pfeffer, J. (1998) Six dangerous myths about pay, *Harvard Business Review*, 76(3), 120; p. 117.

Index

Printed and bound by CPI Group (UK) Ltd, Croydon, CR0 4YY

16/04/2025

14658821-0001